CAKE

ANDREW BAKER

CAKE

A Slice of
British Life

MUDLARK

Mudlark
HarperCollins*Publishers*
1 London Bridge Street
London SE1 9GF

www.harpercollins.co.uk

HarperCollins*Publishers*
Macken House, 39/40 Mayor Street Upper
Dublin 1, D01 C9W8, Ireland

First published by Mudlark 2023

1 3 5 7 9 10 8 6 4 2

A catalogue record of this book is
available from the British Library

ISBN 978-0-00-855607-5

Printed and bound in the UK using 100%
renewable electricity at CPI Group (UK) Ltd

WHEN USING KITCHEN APPLIANCES PLEASE ALWAYS
FOLLOW THE MANUFACTURER'S INSTRUCTIONS

MIX
Paper | Supporting
responsible forestry
FSC
www.fsc.org
FSC™ C007454

This book is produced from independently certified FSC™ paper
to ensure responsible forest management.

For more information visit: www.harpercollins.co.uk/green

For Ingrid

CONTENTS

INTRODUCTION

When was the last time you thought about cake? Probably not long ago. You might have been making a cup of tea, for instance, when it occurred to you that a slice of cake would go very nicely with it. Perhaps you were buying a sandwich to eat at your desk, and you (rightly) felt that a morsel of cake afterwards would make the meal less dispiriting. Or perhaps, as often occurs to me, you were in the middle of some supposedly important project or discussion when the notion of a chunk of cake, or even an entire cake – enticing, plump and pristine – floated unbidden into your mind and lodged there, preventing any further cognitive activity.

These are mundane, everyday (in every sense) cake thoughts.

But when did you last really *think* about cake? When did you last pause before devouring a slice and wonder about where the recipe originated, why it is called what it is called, what the significance of the ingredients might be... what, in cake terms, it all really means?

Perhaps you never have. Perhaps you are happy to simply take cake as it is, without worrying too much about its history or culture or significance.

That's fine. Cake is a pleasure that needs no justification or explanation. Put the book down, ideally before you have smeared it with buttercream or speckled it with crumbs. Because there are serious matters to address here.

Let me explain. I'm very fond of a slice of cake. I find that it lifts my energy levels at mid-morning or mid-afternoon, and lifts the spirits at any time. A slice of cake is more substantial than a boiled sweet, yet less filling than a sandwich; and if the cake is well made it can be a treat for the senses in a much more substantial way than a cup of coffee or tea. I'm not alone in feeling this: an academic study conducted in Manchester found that members of working-class families preferred cake to biscuits, puddings and sweets. Quite right, too.

But an honest slice is hard to come by. A short manifesto follows: if it helps, you can put on some stirring classical music of a vaguely uplifting character, and imagine the author with his chin jutting out in a determined manner, staring into the middle distance with an air of grim resolve.

I believe that as a nation we have lost touch with our cakes. The extraordinary success of *The Great British Bake Off*, for all its cultural cuddliness and culinary expertise, has encouraged baking as an exercise in show-offery, while the programme-maker's hunger for innovation has driven contestants to ever wilder feats of improvisation. The classic Battenberg, for example, was left behind years ago – now, for *GBBO*, it must be a gluten-free chocolate orange Battenberg.

Meanwhile on the high street, the relentless march of the cupcake continues to sweep all before it. There is no shortage of cake shops in British towns and cities, but there is a shortage of cakes within them: windows bedecked with fake flowers frame rows of little pucks of sponge, each sinking under a mini-mountain of sugary buttercream. If you want a grown-up cake for a special occasion you will almost certainly have to choose from minor variants on the American layer cake: slabs of sponge in a cylindrical tower, thickly encased in yet more buttercream. There's cake in there somewhere, but you have to excavate it from beneath slabs of fat and sugar.

It is not true that invention is dead in the cake kitchen – but the delicate triumphs of the pâtissier's art can usually only be found in miniature form at the smartest of hotels, sharing tiered plates with finger sandwiches (the crusts inevitably removed), scones, jam and clotted cream, with a glass of bubbly winking nearby. This will cost around £75 – per person.

This is not a crisis: the cake is not in danger. It's more a state of confusion, in which we are so surrounded by variations on the theme that we have lost track of where the originals came from and what – if anything – they signify. I found myself one day in an upmarket and trendy cake shop, surrounded by huge pastel-hued slabs and thinking: how did we get here?

And as soon as I started to think hard about my favourite cakes the subject unfurled in front of me like a vast tablecloth spread for a gargantuan tea party. So many cakes! So many stories! As I thought of my favourites, I wanted to know more about them – how, when and where did they come into being, why did they include certain ingredients, how did they come by their names?

I realised I had a major project to pursue: an enticing prospect, but one that threatened to spiral rapidly out of control unless I set some boundaries.

I have a family and responsibilities, so I couldn't simply pop some indigestion tablets into a rucksack and set off to sample every cake in the world. It made a lot more sense to restrict myself to cakes that have established a place in British life, acknowledging happily and immediately that in cake, as in so much else, this country has always assimilated delicious ideas and ingredients from far afield.

Not every cake in this book is purely British – that would be a ridiculous and unenforceable restriction; but one of my criteria is that the cakes I feature should be well established in the affections of British eaters. Another characteristic that I wanted to pursue was the stories behind the cakes I chose: so I was looking for cakes with a tale of their own, with some kind of cultural significance and a distinctive character. Cakes whose history I could get my teeth into.

And as the project took shape I realised that simply looking things up and then eating them was not going to suffice. I needed to eat those cakes in the right circumstances.

It's easy enough to send out for cake – or practically any other foodstuff – and I could have assembled the edible elements of this book at home within a couple of days at most. But that would be lazy, gluttonous, self-indulgent and dull. How much more interesting it would be, I thought, to set myself a kind of quest: not only to draw up a list of the cakes that the people of these islands cherish, but to investigate their stories – and then, by way of a challenge, try to eat a chunk of each, as it were the True Slice, in a place appropriate to its story.

It's a kind of culinary version of psychogeography, a way of writing about people, places and things that grew out of the work of radical thinkers, artists and writers in France in the 1950s, and was developed in literary form in Britain by Peter Ackroyd and, in particular, the London walker and writer Iain Sinclair. In very simple terms, psychogeography suggests that places – landscapes, buildings, the underlying territory – shape the behaviour of the people who pass through them. If you have ever come across the stone monuments of a bygone age on a lonely hilltop and shivered, or looked over your shoulder at dusk on a derelict city street to see no one there, you have felt psychogeography at work.

I'm no expert, but I like the idea that a sense of place can enhance the telling of a story, even if the story is only about cakes. So another element was added: I would set out to tell the story of much-loved cakes, and eat each one in a place that was relevant to its story. This plan of action also provided an excuse to escape the kitchen. While I am a Baker by name and love to bake, I'm simply not very good at it, and an account of my misadventures with whisk, oven and piping bag would be as dry and disappointing as one of my overbaked sponges. And while I love to watch people in the kitchen who are much better than me at cooking, there is no shortage of How to Bake books on the market already. It seemed mean-spirited, though, to deny hungry readers who are better bakers than I the chance to have a go, so at the end of each chapter I have supplied a relevant recipe – often with a personal connection.

Sometimes, as you'll see, the choice of location was fairly straightforward: Dundee and Eccles for the cakes named after, and first created, in those communities. Other locations are to do with the history of a cake itself, or of the people who inspired or particularly enjoyed it. Then there are 'occasion' cakes, which prompted their own special places to visit.

My Grand Tour of the cake sites of Britain took about a year to complete, travelling at weekends and on occasional days off from my job in a London newspaper office. Not every trip went according to plan, but if I didn't always locate the cake I was after I certainly learned something every time I set out – even if it was only the early-closing schedule of certain regional bakeries. The quests – even the cakeless ones – were thoroughly enjoyable, because I love to travel, and I love it even more when I travel with a purpose.

I have organised the cake stories and journeys not in the order that I made them, but in something approximating a chronology of the history of cake in British lives. I say 'approximating' because the evolution of cake is not, thank goodness, a Darwinian process: ancient cakes survive alongside modern innovations, and the story of one kind of cake overlaps with that of others. Precisely where in history to locate ginger cake, for example, was not an easy decision. But it seemed to me that there was a clear progression from primitive cakes, to medieval 'great cakes', on to the industrial and marketing innovations of the Victorians and finally to the extravagances, vulgarities – and fun – of the present day.

INTRODUCTION

I hope you enjoy the journeys and the story, and I hope that my book reawakens a hunger for cakes that you once loved and have lost, or cakes that you have yet to meet and love. Baking a cake and sharing it out is an act of love and honour to the recipients: I send this book out into the world in the same spirit. Tuck in and enjoy!

CHAPTER 1
THE FIRST CAKES

Just as every journey of a thousand miles starts with a single step, so every journey of a thousand calories starts with a single bite. Which should be my first cake?

One route of cake exploration leads back to my childhood. Food, as countless writers have pointed out, is a wonderful way to reawaken early memories. I have found, many times, that when entertaining friends a nostalgic element on the table – a bottle of HP Sauce, a packet of Love Hearts sweets, a jam roly-poly served with Bird's custard – will prompt reminiscence and lively conversation.

The most famous example of this in literature is, of course, the madeleine crumbled into a limeflower tisane that sets in motion the one and a quarter million words of Marcel Proust's *À La Recherche du Temps Perdu*. I'm not going to go to Combray, the village in the book, in search of a madeleine, mainly because this is a book about British cakes, but also because Combray is fictional; and Illiers, where Proust actually lived, trades more on the image of the cake than the cakes

11

themselves. I'd also like to point out that according to Proustian scholars, in the first draft of the novel the narrator had his memory stirred by a piece of bread and jam – the madeleine-and-limeflower was suggested by the book's editor.

But the 'madeleine moment' is undoubtedly effective, and I found on many occasions while researching this book that a piece of cake prompted in me, and those I consulted, welcome memories that had remained long hidden.

So which was the first cake for me? I was born in the 1960s, and the first cake-like foods that I can recall are Farley's Rusks, and sponge fingers. My mother, a child of the 1920s who was herself brought up by parents with Victorian values, insists now that both of these items were too luxurious to have been found often in our household, but my memories and sense responses are quite clear: almost certainly they were treats, which would account for the firmness with which they have lodged in my mind.

Firmness is not the texture that I recall in relation to either of these products, though. Sogginess is what comes to mind.

A Farley's Rusk, if you are not familiar with the concept, is a hockey puck of sweet baked nothingness whose primary purpose is to introduce babies to the concept of solid food. The idea – and those who have raised children will almost certainly know this – is that the friable rusk breaks easily even in a toothless mouth into crumbs that dissolve. The high sugar content (it is the second named ingredient, after wheat flour and before palm oil) ensures that baby rapidly learns to associate solid food with a sugar rush – and comes back for more.

I remember clearly as a young child – not a toothless baby, but not far beyond toddlerhood – eating a Farley's Rusk with milk. The rusk sat in the base of a small bowl which was decorated with incidents from the exciting life of Peter Rabbit. My mother would pour a little milk around the rusk and hand me my spoon, and my great delight was carving off little chunks that combined a top layer of crisp golden crust with the soft, white, sodden crumb beneath.

Some childhood food memories can have me scuttling to the store cupboard or the high street for a rapid reprise. This is not one of them. But the other memory I have from around this era, formed in the little kitchen of our old house at Hadley Highstone near Barnet, just north of London, is both closer to cake and closer to appetising.

Sponge fingers, as they are known to the British, are not only one of my oldest food memories but also one of the earliest forms of cake as we now think of it. In the easiest assignment of this entire project, I have just walked around the corner to our nearest branch of Tesco and bought some, an action that for the outlay of £1.15 brings me instantly closer to my childhood – and to 500 years of baking history.

They are fairly basic items, frosted digits with the rigidity of a biscuit and the inner give of a cake. Their origin story, quoted in umpteen sources with sometimes outlandish embellishments, is worth recounting because it marks a plausible and significant development in the evolution of the cake from something like a biscuit to something more like the cake we know and love today.

Sponge fingers (ladyfingers in the USA, many other names of varying degrees of decency elsewhere) are popularly supposed to have been first created at the court of the Count of Savoy, in what is now France, in the fourteenth century. Amadeus VI of Savoy, so the story goes, was expecting Charles IV of Luxembourg for dinner and asked his chef, a man called Pierre de Yenne, to prepare a cake 'as light as a feather.'

To achieve this, de Yenne beat together egg yolks and sugar for a long time, getting as much air as possible into the mixture, before folding in beaten egg white. At some point there must have been some flour involved as well (these days in Savoie they use potato flour). The result was a sponge of remarkable purity and lightness, and the method, chiefly employing nothing more than the heft of the cook to impart air – and therefore lift – into the mixture, was little changed for the preparation of sponge cakes until the invention and industrialisation of raising agents in the nineteenth century.

The man most instrumental in the development of the modern sponge cake – to which we will return in another chapter – also has a key part to play in my childhood enjoyment of sponge fingers.

Because Alfred Bird (of whom more on page 95), who popularised the baking powder that lifts sponge, was also the King of Custard, glorious accompaniment to the sponge finger.

In the kitchen at Hadley Highstone, I had progressed from Farley's Rusks further up the food chain to sponge fingers and custard. Not in a trifle, which is the customary arrangement of these two components, further adorned for adult consumption with a sprinkle of sherry, some fruit jelly and lashings of cream. No, that would have been decadent in the extreme.

Instead the young Bakers, myself and my little brother James, were presented on special occasions with a bowl of Bird's custard, steaming and golden, and a pair of sponge fingers – each! – to dip in it.

This seemed to us then a heavenly indulgence, and the fact that when I mentioned it recently to my now elderly mother she denied all knowledge of it suggests that it must have been a rare treat indeed. My mother says now that she would never have spoilt us in this way, and can only suppose that it was *her* mother, on occasion left in sole charge of the two little boys, who may have cut loose in this lavish manner.

Certainly it was my grandmother who used to delight in telling us tales of the scarcely imaginable wealth and extravagance of Mr Bird. While she stirred his bright yellow custard powder into a saucepan on the hob, and James and I drummed our little spoons on the kitchen table, Grandma would say, 'Mr Bird lives in a mansion, and all his servants wear uniforms the colour of his custard.' Then she'd bring the saucepan to the table, and carefully pour out a pool of smooth, steaming gloop into each of our bowls.

And as we dipped our sponge fingers into the divine mixture, and then blew on them because hot custard is very dangerous, she would tell us for the twentieth time about Mr Bird's Rolls-Royce, 'painted bright yellow, just like the custard in your bowls, so that when he drives through town, everyone knows who he is.'

I loved that image, an early notion of what success and fame might look like. One day, I thought, I too will drive through town in a colourful Rolls-Royce and everyone will know who I am. It's yet to happen.

It struck me now, writing all of this down, that my grandmother might have made it all up. Elsie Martin – of whom more later in the book – came originally from the East End of London, and retained many of the characteristics for which the women of that neighbourhood are rightly celebrated: she was tough; no-nonsense; forthright in expression. But also occasionally given to telling what in the slang of her childhood home are called 'pork pies'.

So I looked up the Bird family and their Rolls-Royce, and found that not only had my grandmother been telling the truth, she had, if anything, underestimated the plutocratic excesses of the baking- and custard-powder dynasty. According to the BBC, the Birds kept not just one custard-yellow Rolls-Royce, but a fleet of them. 'Fancy that...' as my grandmother would have said.

Farley's Rusks and sponge fingers – both purchased, I'm sure, in the modest Barnet High Street branch of Sainsbury's, a short bus ride from Hadley Highstone – comprise my earliest memories that are related to cake.

They take us back to the mid-1960s, and the sponge fingers, as we have seen, take the origins of the modern notion of cake back to the medieval era. How much further back does the history of cake go, and how close can I get to the ancient British original?

I fall back on family assistance once again, in a way.

In old age (she is ninety-eight as I type these words) but robust good health, my mother lives now in a retirement community in a village on the border between Oxfordshire and Berkshire. I often visit at the weekend, and stop off en route in the nearest town to buy whatever supplies she needs.

The town is Wantage, not a great centre of the cake industry but strongly associated with King Alfred the Great, who was born there in the year 849 ('Not long before me,' as my mother has often pointed out).

A statue of this notable monarch presides over the town square and is always in the corner of one's eye when scuttling from shop to shop. It's not a very good statue – it was executed by a relative of Queen Victoria and is regularly vandalised – but it popped into my mind when I was thinking about the history of cake in this country.

Alfred was a remarkable monarch in many ways. Although King of Wessex rather than of England, he did more than any ruler before him to unite the future nation, while fending off the Danes, or the Vikings, or both, and doing his best to educate his people in matters of law, heritage and religion.

Yet if the subjects of his modern successor know anything at all about him, it is that he burnt the cakes. And if they know anything at all about cakes, they know that the items that King Alfred burnt were not cakes as we understand the term today.

The story may be myth, legend, apocryphal or entirely fiction – it was first written down about 100 years after it was supposed to have taken place – but to me it has the ring of truth. For a start, it does not depict the king in any kind of heroic or glorious light, and it does not take place in a grand or martial setting. It has charm, and humour, and is just that kind of quirky incident, minor yet revealing of character, that might first have been passed on as fireside gossip before achieving wider currency.

Whatever the truth, the story goes that in the late ninth century, Alfred had been leading his followers in a series of battles with a large Danish raiding force in the West Country, and between skirmishes retreated to the Somerset Levels, where one day the battle-weary king sought refuge in the humble hut of a swineherd and his wife, who were unaware of his real identity.

As the king rested by the fire, the little cakes of kneaded flour which the swineherd's wife had placed in the embers burnt while she was attending to other domestic matters, and she berated her guest for watching them burn instead of attending them. You'll be happy enough to eat them, she forth-rightly pointed out, but you couldn't be bothered to get up and turn them.

I know the shops, restaurants and cafés of Wantage pretty well, and I have never found a King Alfred's Cake on sale anywhere in the town. This is a missed marketing opportunity – others, including English Heritage, have not hesitated – but it may also reflect that fact that no one really knows what kind of culinary creation Alfred's absent-mindedness caused to burn.

CRUMBS OF KNOWLEDGE
THE WORD 'CAKE'

Not only is it challenging to pin down the early history of cake in this country, it is hard to establish the origins of the word itself. It is first recorded in the correct context in what is recognisably modern English in the late fourteenth century, but how it came into the language is not entirely clear.

Commentators with varying degrees of academic credibility claim confidently that the word came into English via Scandinavian settlers and their Old Norse word *kaka*, meaning lump or clod – as it were of snow, or mud. In this case the word is describing the shape of the thing – in much the same way that we now describe a cake of soap – rather than describing something which is cooked, or which has a certain taste.

This is perfectly plausible, and would provide a nice historical irony by suggesting that the things King Alfred burnt would come to be known by a name taken from the language of his enemies.

But it also seems possible that, instead, the word cake survived, corrupted, from the Roman occupation of Britain and came into the language via Old and Middle English as a variant of the Latin *cocus*, the cook.

We may never know the truth. But alongside this ancient etymology it is interesting to note that one of the most recent recruits to the English language is also cake-related.

The term, admitted to the *Oxford English Dictionary*'s New Words List in December 2020, is 'cakeage', analogous to corkage and relating to the charge levied by a restaurant for cutting and serving a cake that has been brought in by a customer.

As far as I can tell, the earliest texts suggest that the swineherd's wife was cooking kneaded flour in some form or another, so the closest modern approximation may be a flatbread or oatcake.

But a Nairn's Oatcake, available in your local Waitrose, might be an acceptable middle-class modern approximation. Ingredients: oats, some kind of binding fat, hint of salt. All available to your average Anglo-Saxon, though archaeologists and food historians often speculate that the oats found on ancient sites might well have been fed (in southern Britain, at least) to animals rather than humans, while the latter employed spelt flour for food purposes. No doubt farming and cooking practices varied from region to region.

A grain of some kind bound with fat of some kind – almost certainly bacon fat, given the profession of her husband – was a perfectly plausible form of baked goods for a swineherd's wife to have cooking in the embers of her fire.

So, on the way down to my nearest authentic Anglo-Saxon dwelling, I stopped at a little Waitrose and scored some Nairn's. The 'Rough' ones, for added ruggedness and primitivity. Now, all I needed was a swineherd's wife.

No such luck: no swine, either, at Butser Ancient Farm, on a chilly Hampshire hillside. But lack of swine was its only failing.

Butser is a wonderful example of the thriving concept of experimental archaeology, where experts not only dig things up, but attempt as far as possible to recreate objects – from simple tools and clothes to entire dwellings – of which only ancient traces remain.

Just over half a century ago, a man called Peter Reynolds started to build ancient houses here, and to experiment with ancient farming techniques and technologies.

I entered prehistory here through the gift shop – racks of mead and slabs of disappointingly modern fruit cake – but once out of the retail experience, the sights, sounds and smells of very olde England were all around me.

My objective was a Saxon Hall at the end of Butser's trail through time, but surely there was no harm in poking around a bit in the preceding centuries. Who knows? I might even come across a cake older than King Alfred's.

No such luck in the Mesolithic, unfortunately, which seemed to consist of little more than a tatty windbreak and an entirely extinguished fire. But there were signs of life issuing from the Neolithic hut – woodsmoke, and chatter.

'Come in, come in, and come close to my fire...' I did as I was bidden, and through the gloom in a roughly thatched hut the size of a double garage I made out a woman in a nightie with what might have been handlebars on her head.

'I am the deer queen!' she pronounced, and while she didn't spell it out I realised that she meant deer (and not dear) because those were probably antlers on her head rather than handlebars.

'Gather round the fire and I shall share with you the secrets of beeswax candles,' the deer queen said.

I realised that I was not alone. There were several families in the hut, all in modern dress – thank goodness – and all consisting of parents trying to get young children to sit down and make candles, while the children had other ideas.

'I want to go home!' a toddler exclaimed, and I made my excuses and left. You can't eat beeswax.

In the centre of the site was a re-created Iron Age village, and in the largest circular hut, perhaps fifteen metres across, a splendid log fire glowed on the central hearth. Around it a dozen or so parents and smallish children were intent on little tasks. Perhaps, I thought, they are preparing little Iron Age cakes in case a hungry wandering scribe should happen upon their clan?

Nope. They were either making little Viking twirly things (dreamcatchers? Troll frighteners?) out of scraps of wool, an exercise that one parent noted under their breath was 'going to take bloody ages', or else writing notes on cards attached to bits of string that could be tied on to a tree that looked very much like but definitely wasn't a Christmas tree, since that would have been epoch-inappropriate, but had instead been designated a Wishing Tree.

I thought of writing a note imploring the pagan gods for a little bit of ancient cake, but the children had taken all the crayons.

So instead I pushed on through time, and across a field, to the Anglo-Saxon compound, where two rather splendid hall houses, each rectangular, steeply thatched and about the size of a squash court, brought me up to roughly the time and housing style of King Alfred.

In the first one a lady in ancient costume, i.e. strategically modified blankets, sat at a trestle table instructing children on the construction of leafy crowns or green garlands, which little ones would then perch atop their heads for a photograph before asking if there was any food.

There wasn't any food. I had a look on the blazing hearth, but it was entirely cake-free, and I enquired of the gentleman standing next to it, dressed from head to foot in plastic holly and with his face painted bright green, if there was any Anglo-Saxon grub on the go.

'No, sorry, not today,' he said. 'But you can get a slice of fruit cake in the gift shop.'

I thanked him, and complimented him on the outfit.

'I'm the Holly King, you see,' he explained.

I said that made a lot of sense, given his outfit.

'I rule for half the year, until the feast of Beltane, and then the Oak King takes over. Or it might be the other way round. It depends who you ask.'

I said that was very interesting. And did he know the Deer Queen?

'Oh yes. She's my missus.'

Well, it takes all sorts, I thought, wishing him a good day.

Next door, like a pair of detached houses on an ancient Barratt development, stood another Anglo-Saxon hall of similar dimensions but built using slightly different methods.

Don't ask me which methods, because I wasn't concentrating on the wattle and thatch.

I was gripped by the fact that (a) this hall also had a fire in its central hearth, and (b) this hall was entirely free from people dressed as hedges, and indeed free from anyone apart from myself.

Excellent.

The stage was thus set for me to recreate the burning of the cakes by King Alfred, with myself in the regal role, and a Nairn's Rough Oatcake in the role of swineherd's wife's cookie.

Reckoning that we could take the scenario as read and do without the initial dialogue – and also lacking anyone to talk to – I cut straight to the crucial scene.

The hearth occupied a low platform of mud brick about the size and height of a coffee table in the middle of the room. The fire, which took up most of the surface, was nicely settled – grey embers glowing around a single smoking log, with just gentle wafts of (very cold) breeze through the wide doorway to encourage an occasional little flicker of flame.

I took four oatcakes from the box and arranged three of them in the embers around the edge of the fire, perching another on top of the log, just for the hell of it. Then I settled on one of the low wooden benches next to the hearth, drew my cloak (from, er, Uniqlo) around me, closed my eyes and tried to think kingly thoughts.

What would have been on King Alfred's mind? Methods of Dane-harrying? War-chariot upgrades? Perhaps he was just tired and hungry. I had got up at the crack of dawn to drive to the farm, and had no breakfast, so I could relate to that. I closed my eyes.

'Excuse me?' I came to and sat bolt upright. A lady in blan-ket-based ancient dress – a volunteer, rather than a swineherd's wife – was standing in the doorway. 'I'm sorry, but you'll have to take those things off the fire. There's a notice there...' She spun on her heel and departed.

How embarrassing. There was indeed a notice, which I hadn't seen, propped up against one side of the hearth plat-form, which said quite clearly in modern English, 'Do NOT put anything on the fire.' Not, 'Please, Your Majesty...', just 'Do NOT...'

Mindful of burning myself, I flicked the oatcakes out of the embers. Two were authentically burned across half their surface, one was totally carbonised, and the one which had been sitting on the log was just nice and warm.

This last one I ate, slowly and ruminatively.

It tasted of smoke and woodchips and very little else, and had the texture of dry porridge. In King Alfred's place, I would have looked for somewhere else to sleep – and eat.

But in the Saxon hut, for all the glaring inaccuracies of dress and compromises on ingredients, I had got fairly close to the essential elements of the first great English cake story. I had learned that the meaning of the word, and the nature of the items defined by the word, had changed drastically over time, and I had begun to understand that cake often helps to reveal character – that of the trustworthy hostess trusting a stranger to watch over them, and that of the brave but fallible monarch who let them burn.

As for the short-sighted farm visitor and the busybody volunteer, you can draw your own conclusions.

I left the Saxon era behind with a cookbook from the gift shop, and considerable relief. My next cakes would come from several hundred years later and a couple of hundred miles north. They would still not be close to the sumptuous creations of the twenty-first century, but they had to taste a whole lot better than King Alfred's burnt offerings.

ANGLO-SAXON OATCAKES

The first recipe in the book is also the only recipe in the book that is mine. But it is only mine in the sense that I have adapted it from other recipes to suit myself, my regular eaters, my limited abilities, and my kitchen.

I don't feel too bad about this: all cake recipes, not just this one but all the others in the book, and all cake recipes since the dawn of recorded history, are versions of other people's recipes.

So, of course, you can modify this one: according to experts in historic cookery, Anglo-Saxons would have made their basic cakes with whichever types of grain and embellishments there were to hand. I have ambitiously assumed a gift of cinnamon, from a wealthy visitor with foreign connections...

THE FIRST CAKES

NOTE: In this, and all the recipes that follow, timings and oven temperatures should be treated with caution. As King Alfred found, and all bakers know, a cake is a capricious creation, and every oven is subtly different.

MAKES 12 LITTLE CAKES

125g unsalted butter
4 large tbsp honey
250g oats, crushed or cut (porridge oats are fine)
1 level tsp ground cinnamon
50g dried apples, chopped

1. Preheat your oven to 180°C/350°F/Gas Mark 4.
2. Melt the butter in a saucepan, then remove from the heat. Add the honey, stir, then add the oats, spice and dried fruit to the melted butter and honey and stir again well until all is properly mixed.
3. Smear a little more butter on a baking tray, spoon 12 dollops of the mixture on it and then flatten them slightly.
4. Bake in the oven for 10–12 minutes. Do not doze off while contemplating military strategy.
5. Place the cakes on a rack to cool. They are good with goat's cheese.

CHAPTER 2
ECCLES

Somehow or another, whether by way of the invading Norsemen or by inheritance from the invading Romans, the name 'cake' became attached to the objects that the king burnt and stayed attached as the story travelled down the centuries, first told by the fireside, then recorded on parchment and in book and on film.

And there are many other cooked items that are still called cake today that bear no relation to the fluffy, golden, risen and gloriously adorned items that we commonly think of when we hear the term.

How to bridge the gap of many centuries – the Dark Ages of Cake – between the ember-cooked oatcakes of the Anglo-Saxons and King Alfred, and the scientifically raised and architecturally adorned extravagances of the Victorians? Where could I find cakes that people had regarded as treats, had treasured for the special days in their calendar... had named after their communities, all before the luxuries of sugar and raising agents and colouring became commonly available?

31

I wanted to find a cake to stand for all these, to represent in my story the different, often ancient, culinary representatives of the wider cake family. Not so extreme as a Pontefract or Pomfrey cake – a lump of liquorice – but perhaps a Welsh cake, cooked on a griddle, so not unrelated to Alfred's hearth cakes... or a Banbury cake, unrisen but adorned with dried fruit... or several of that ilk that are survivors from the simple bakes created in Pre-Reformation England to celebrate saints' days, for centuries the best excuse that the calendar offered for a feast.

It wasn't very hard. There are dozens of them, mostly variations on a very simple theme. When I talked to friends about this book in its early stages the exchange would often go something like:

> Me: *'I'm writing a book about cake, actually.'*
> Friend: *'Cake, eh? You'll have to include my local favourite.'*
> Me: *'I'd be delighted to. What is it?'*
> Friend: *'Sprocklington cake! It's medieval.'*
> Me: *'Fascinating. What's it like?'*
> Friend: *'Hmm. Sort of currants in pastry, really...'*

If you ever find yourself unexpectedly in possession of a stall at a farmer's market, all you need to stock it is a supply of currants and some pastry (any pastry – you can make up the back-story later). Combine currants and pastry in a slightly weird way: folded into triangles, for instance, or glazed with duck-egg yolk, or shaped into runic symbols, call them [Name of Town] cakes and invent a story about how they were first baked to celebrate the feast of [insert name of obscure saint] and you can't lose. They'll sell like... they'll sell very well.

Inventing my own would be cheating, though. Instead I looked through umpteen recipes and 'curious histories' and narrowed the list down to two of the most celebrated of these old-style pastry cakes, the Eccles cake, with Banbury a close second, the latter sometimes containing spice and citrus peel, the former sometimes without; both to be consumed, my conscience demanded, on an appropriate spot.

The Eccles cake must be the most famous of these confections, created in and named after a village long subsumed into the urban sprawl of Manchester and still celebrated there, but also adored by chefs and foodies much further afield.

One such is Fergus Henderson, a friend of mine from childhood and the wonderful, eccentric and inspiring creator of the St John restaurant in London. Fergus champions simple, robust food that combines fine ingredients in powerful ways, and one of his favourite combinations, present for many years on his menus, is an Eccles cake with Lancashire cheese.

I might have gone to St John and shared a plate with him, but while the prospect was alluring it would also have been cheating: my questing rules demand that I seek out an authentic version of each cake in a place appropriate to it. And while Fergus is many things he is not Mancunian, and the Eccles cake comes not from Farringdon in central London, but Eccles in the city of Salford, a few miles west of central Manchester. Also, slightly peculiarly, the Eccles cakes served at St John are vegetarian, which can hardly be said for much of the menu at that famously carnivorous restaurant, while most Mancunians hold that butter – and perhaps also lard – have their place in the pastry.

The Eccles cake – like the other cakes in this chapter – is related to religion. But not because it is associated with a particular festival, like the Simnel cake of Easter or the Twelfth Cake of Christmas.

It's all in the name – because the town of Eccles takes its name from a church that stood at the centre of the community in its earliest days – or at least from the twelfth century. The Eccles cake, like Eccles the village, is eccles as in ecclesiastic, or to do with the church, from the Greek *ecclesia*, meaning an assembly.

That makes the Eccles cake an especially appropriate representative of its kind, the little curranty cakes associated in the distant past with religious feast days. An early literary reference comes from Chaucer, who mentioned one – the 'God's kichel' in 'The Summoner's Tale'. This seems to have been a little triangular pastry involving currants, handed out at Christmas and by godparents to their godchildren.

Chaucer's word may derive, according to the blogger The Old Foodie, from the Anglo-Saxon *cicel*, meaning a small mouthful; the relationship, if any, to the Yiddish word *kichel* – meaning cookie – is one for philologists.

The Coventry godcake is the only blatantly religious British survivor, a puff pastry triangle stuffed with mincemeat (i.e. mince-pie filling) and supposed to be made by godparents to be served at christenings. The triangle represents the Holy Trinity, and I'd have tried to find an authentic example but felt it would be a bit weird to tout around for invitations to other people's christenings a long way from where I live.

Eccles cakes belong to the same culinary family and are accessible without gate-crashing family church services. Off to Manchester then...

I caught the tram out to Eccles from central Manchester. Not without difficulty, for the city's transport team threw my meticulous preparations up in the air by closing some of the direct route that I had planned. But I'm a Londoner, which brings two benefits in this kind of situation: one is that I am very used to being messed around with on public transport, and the other is that I welcome the excuse to improvise, wander around and explore a city that is relatively unknown to me.

I couldn't get anywhere from Piccadilly Gardens, as planned, so I trudged a little way in the direction I had come from back to Market Street, where I waited for a while at the tram stop next to the comprehensively defunct Debenhams department store, already speckled with lively and apocalyptic graffiti. From there I caught a double tram to Deansgate, where I waited a further ten minutes in what was by now driving drizzle for the Eccles tram.

By my original calculations I should already have been at my destination, surrounded by enthusiastic artisan bakers offering their wares. Never mind. Quests are not meant to be easy.

The Eccles tram didn't go straight to Eccles, either: it trundled first to Salford Quays and MediaCity UK, a chunk of redeveloped dockside next to the old ship canal, now home to northern outposts of the BBC and ITV and a few high-rise residential developments.

At the MediaCityUK stop half a dozen trendy young folk got off and nobody got on. The driver abandoned his cab at one end of the tram, sauntered down the car and climbed into an identical cab at the other end, from which he steered us out – at last – on to the final leg of the journey to Eccles.

It's the end of the line now, a distant suburb of the big city. But it has a cake of its own, a culinary echo of the time when this was a self-contained town, an independent community half a day's ride from Manchester. I tried to picture that proud town now: the old church loomed, dark with ancient soot, through the drizzle, and the high street comprised pubs, bookmakers and closed shutters, interspersed with one or two enterprising outlets selling buckets, mops and plastic flowers.

I had a feeling, as I stepped off the tram, that this was unlikely to be artisan bakery territory.

Even this early in my Cake Quest, I was developing rudimentary antennae for likely bakers and makers, and Eccles didn't seem like the right spot for either. But there was no denying the heritage, and I felt honour bound to explore as I considered the story.

The Eccles cake, most sources concur, was originally associated with the feast day of St Mary, dedicatee of the old church, which kicked off three days of celebrations, the Eccles Wakes, in August. Over time, and despite the efforts of the Puritans to ban anything pleasurable that was associated with religion, the little cakes of dried fruit in pastry gained a wider following.

Elizabeth Raffald, a Manchester resident, gave a recipe for 'sweet patties' – very reminiscent of Eccles cakes – in her 1769 cookbook, *The Experienced English Housekeeper*, and in 1796 one James Birch is recorded making and selling the cakes in a shop opposite the church.

Soon, travellers were coming from far and wide to stock up on the local delicacy, and the compilers of an 1838 guide to the railways of the Midlands and North noted that the 'little town is famous for its cakes'. There's a lovely old photograph of a little shop called Ye Olde Thatche, which purports to have been built in 1099 and which sells, according to the signwriting, herb beer, cigars, and the 'Real old original Eccles cakes'.

Unfortunately Ye Olde Thatche fell to ye olde demolition men in 1915 and was replaced by a bank, which was now shut.

James Birch's shop is gone too, replaced by Freddy's Chicken and Pizza, which was also shut. The only bakery of any kind on the high street was Greggs, which I entered with a heavy heart and left less than a minute later with the briskly acquired knowledge that they do NOT sell Eccles cakes.

Greggs is in the pedestrianised centre of the little town, adjoining a Sixties brick piazza of some bleakness. There were shuttered shops, and one or two charity outlets, on three sides of the low-built square; the fourth was occupied by a branch of Wilko, the bargain homewares chain. In the middle of the paved central space, where in Milan or Milton Keynes there might be a spouting fountain or challenging sculpture, there stood a substantial and blatantly artificial Christmas tree. Propped up against it in unnatural poses, stiff and staring-eyed as if in the aftermath of a terrible massacre, were two life-sized plastic reindeer. Santa was nowhere to be seen – reasonably enough, in mid-November.

Instead of Christmas cheer there was bingo – a determinedly upbeat lady outside the coffee shop next to Wilko had a number-generating gadget and a microphone, and was calling out the vital digits to half a dozen well-wrapped customers and their grumpy dogs sheltering from the drizzle at a row of little tables set up against the redundant shop-fronts.

No Eccles cakes. I wandered through the pedestrianised zone and out on to the high street once more.

The only businesses that were clearly thriving were the pubs. This may not accurately reflect the lifestyle choices of the inhabitants: in cold and driving drizzle, conversations that might otherwise take place on a street corner are better held indoors. In the Nag's Head, whose sign depicted a fearsome matron with a rolling pin, men for whom she might have been waiting at home were gathered convivially around their mid-morning pints.

I walked up the street to the church of St Mary the Virgin, a substantial edifice that retained an atmospheric layer of nineteenth-century grime. I was keen to see inside, but all the doors were locked and against one of them was a pile of dead cans of Stella Artois lager. On the wall beside the main door a banner flapped damply, inviting all to 'a free warm drink, a biscuit and a friendly chat'... perhaps even an Eccles cake... but the welcome was available only on Thursdays at 2pm, and I couldn't hang around for three days on the off-chance.

Plodding back towards the transport interchange I was suddenly struck by a wonderful sight – a giant Eccles cake!

Only two-dimensional, to be sure, but a sign that I was, after all, in the right place. The mural of Eccles life, vertical rather than horizontal, took up the entire side wall of a (closed) corner shop. At the top of the lively painting, children rode on swans. In the centre of the image, foolish folk wrestled an energetic bull, and all of the foreground, closest to street level, was occupied with bakers carrying trays laden with Eccles cakes.

With such encouragement it would have been wrong to give up. Two options remained, both of them a cop-out: Aldi and Morrisons.

The latter was beside the tram stop and I marked it down as my last chance saloon. Aldi was behind a boarded-up pub, the Albert Edward, with a discoloured sign of Edward VII, looking suitably grim, swinging in the breeze.

Aldi was – I'm not going to waste time describing Aldi. It was like all the other Aldis, brightly lit and rammed with packets that looked very much like packets that hold nice things, but which turn out on closer inspection to be imitations of those packets, containing imitations of nice things.

I couldn't find any Eccles cakes, so I asked a lady who was stacking packs of toilet roll called something like Androx.

'Oh, you want Morning Goods, love,' she said. 'Next aisle along.'

Under a vast sign announcing 'Morning Goods' (am I alone in never having heard that phrase before? It means fresh from the bakery that morning, so was only partially truthful in this context) was an array of baked things in plastic wrapping.

I noticed, with a creeping sense of irony and irritation, versions of a number of cakes that I planned to find elsewhere

(Victoria slices, Battenberg, Jamaica ginger) and I was starting to think that I might save a lot of time and trouble by simply settling down with my notebook and writing the whole book here.

Then I saw Chorley cakes... and next to them – Eccles cakes! A brief moment of elation, and then a great sense of anti-climax, rather as King Arthur might have felt, after a hard morning's questing, coming across the Holy Grail among the colanders in Wilko.

But here I was in Eccles, with 'Real Lancashire Eccles Cakes Containing Pure Butter'. I scored two packs, and a pack of Chorley cakes too. Mission – sort of – accomplished.

I had a hunch that Morrisons – being a north-country supermarket chain, rather than a German interloper – might do a better job with the local specialities, so I headed over there and sure enough, in the bakery section at the back, discovered not only more Real Lancashire Eccles Cakes, but some that had been Baked In-Store Today. Much greater in circumference than the Aldi versions, too, more on the scale of Eccles mini-pizzas.

Right. Fully caked-up. Now... where to eat them? En route to Manchester I had imagined that I would find in Eccles a community largely revolving around happy bakers and their delicious wares, to be consumed perhaps on open tables in the cobbled streets while colourful locals shared cake-related tales with me of their harsh yet picturesque childhoods.

None of this had come to pass. The cakes were in a super-market bag, the streets weren't cobbled and the locals were in the pub. Yet in honour of my concept and through a warped sense of duty, I felt I had to consume Eccles cakes while still in Eccles. I was drawn back to the church. It was still locked but there was a lychgate with a neat tiled roof giving shelter from the drizzle.

With the old church behind me I unwrapped my cakes – the Aldi package first – and took a bite.

No blinding light blazed down from the heavens. Try as I might, gazing through the precipitation at the site of James Birch's original Eccles cake bakery, I could not summon the spirit or savour of olden days. All I saw was Freddy's Chicken and Pizza, and all I tasted was cardboardy pastry and a currant or two.

Morrison's cake was not a great deal better – though bigger, and crunchier – but altogether that experience was thoroughly un-transcendental. I headed off to the tram stop, in need of a new plan.

Local insight was required. Fortunately, my tram route back into town required a change at Deansgate, where my favourite Manchester foodies hung out. A quick exchange of texts while the tram rumbled along established that a warm welcome awaited me at Dormouse Chocolate, two minutes' walk from the tram stop.

Dormouse – which I heartily recommend to anyone visiting the city – is a combination of shop and artisanal chocolate factory, where life and business partners Karen and Isobel make wonderful, multi-award-winning craft chocolate bars and sell their wares and those of other British craft chocolate makers.

The shop was closed to the public that day – hours are limited to fit in with chocolate production – but Isobel was there slaving over an array of vats, grinders and tempering slabs. I'd outlined my quest by text and she had already been in touch with like-minded souls to seek out the city's finest Eccles cakes ('not necessarily from Eccles,' I had added, having exhausted that area).

As an expression of goodwill – and also because I adore their work – I bought several bars of fine Dormouse chocolate, and Isobel gave me a taster of an upcoming bar blending white chocolate with ginger, spices and candied peel. It was heavenly...

But not my goal. 'You need to go to Failsworth,' Isobel declared. 'Robinson's Family Bakers. Everyone says they make the best Eccles cakes in Manchester.'

Baked on the premises? I asked.

'Definitely,' Isobel said. 'They're up the Oldham Road.'

'Jolly good,' I said, assuming, the way that non-residents of cities often do, that everything is just around the corner. 'Can I pop round there on foot?' Isobel looked doubtful. 'Tram?'

'Well,' she said, still looking doubtful, 'you might try a bus. It's quite a way...'

The obvious thing to do, of course, would have been to ring a taxi from the warm, dry, chocolatey surroundings of Dormouse. But that only occurred to me after I had been walking for five minutes or so through drizzle that was turning by degrees into determined rain. It also occurred to me that I had no idea which bus I was looking for, or even what means of payment would be required should I ever find the right one.

Outside the Midland Hotel a lone taxi stood on the stand. Without giving the driver any excuse to decline my custom, I climbed aboard.

'Robinson's Artisan Family Bakery,' I stated.

'Never heard of it,' the driver said.

Ashton Road East, I told him, firmly, and we set off.

Because it was cold, and rainy, and the taxi was warm, the windows quickly fogged up and I couldn't either open them a little or work out how the air blower worked. So I was reduced to wiping myself little portholes from time to time to work out where we were.

Through one of them I caught the nameplate of Every Street, but it might have been Any Street for all my knowledge of the fringes of Manchester. Unfortunately the driver, whose name according to the sticker on the glass divider was Rahim, had little more idea of where to go than I did.

'This isn't working,' he admitted, working on a three-point turn in a cul-de-sac in what as far as I could tell from the fringes of the windows was some kind of industrial estate. 'Have you got a postcode?'

I fiddled around with my phone, found it and relayed it to Rahim, who tapped it into his Satnav, which immediately started to issue instructions in a tone that suggested admonishment.

Eventually we found the wrong end of the right street, turned around, looked about, and halted in front of Robinson's. The lights were on, but the sign on the door said 'Closed' and a lady in a hygienic hat was draping paper sheets over the baked products in the window display.

Closed?

It was twenty past two on a Monday afternoon – and by this time I was out of the taxi and tapping insistently on the shop door. The lady shook her head. I pantomimed desperation, and she came over and unlocked the door.

'Please,' I begged. 'Let me in. I have to get some Eccles cakes.'

'But we're shut.'

'You don't understand,' I said. 'I've come from London especially for some of your Eccles cakes.'

'Well – let me talk to the boss,' she said, shutting the door in my face. But gently. I gave Rahim a tentative thumbs-up, but his window was fogged up and he didn't see me. He hadn't been paid yet, so he wasn't going anywhere.

Soon a middle-aged lady arrived, also wearing a hygienic hat.

'Come in out of the rain,' she said, adding, 'We're shut, you know.'

Let's cut to the chase. 'Please tell me,' I said. 'Do you have any of your lovely hand-made Eccles cakes left?'

She bustled behind the counter and peered under the relevant sheet of protective paper. 'Yes. Two.'

'I'll take them.'

They couldn't take cash because the till was locked and it was all a bit irregular, but I paid with my card – it was less than two pounds – and thanked the lady fulsomely, explaining again that I had come a long way specially for their cakes.

'But why did you come all this way?' the lady asked.

'My friend told me to,' I explained.

'Do you always do everything that your friends tell you to?' she asked, showing me out of the door. 'You'll get into trouble one day.'

Rahim seemed relieved at my return, probably because there was no way he would have seen me through his steamed-up windows doing a runner if I had; and he was even more relieved when he heard – and recognised – my destination: Manchester Piccadilly Station.

The train back down south was rammed, and the seat next to me – and a fair proportion of my own seat – was occupied by a substantial middle management type with a laptop and unruly elbows.

But I didn't mind. Earlier in the day, in a little branch of Waitrose near the chocolate shop, I had bought a small pack of Mrs Kirkham's Lancashire cheese, and on my way through the station I had acquired a wooden knife from Pret.

As the train pulled out of Piccadilly, I cleared a little space on the bit of my tray table unoccupied by the middle manager's elbow. There I marshalled one of my Robinson's Eccles cakes – a lovely, plump creation, with dark fruit visible through the slash on top – and a couple of chunks of Mrs Kirkham's finest, and tucked in.

I sat an oblong of cheese the size of an old book of matches atop the generous curve of the cake, which had the dimensions of a squashed cricket ball. The pastry was golden with caramelised sugar, and when I chomped down on cheese and cake the combination disintegrated wonderfully in my mouth, scattering simple, robust flavours: sweet sugar, sharp fruit, tangy cheese, underpinned by the buttery base note of the pastry.

It was tremendously satisfying: not sophisticated or luxurious, but a combination that had evolved through time to do a thoroughly efficient job. It didn't surprise me in the least that Fergus of St John, perhaps my generation's finest judge of English food, rates this pairing so highly.

As the train gathered speed I raised my cake in benediction once in the direction of Eccles, a mile to the right through the window, and once in the general direction of Fergus in London. Then I popped another little slablet of cheese into place and tucked in once more.

It was good, and I felt satisfied not simply with the taste experience but also that I had made a genuine effort to eat an Eccles cake in Eccles. It rankled a little that the finest cake had not come from Eccles exactly – and had, in all honesty, been consumed when moving past Eccles at a steadily increasing velocity. But perhaps I would be able to tick my self-imposed boxes with more accuracy in Banbury.

Fully aware from my research that there were many communities in Britain that boasted their own versions of these basic fruit and pastry 'cakes', I felt I ought to try at least one variation on the theme. I had a Chorley cake, another Lancashire confection purchased in the Eccles Aldi, but it looked like an Eccles cake that had been run over by a tram and tasted like that too. No disrespect to the people of Chorley, but greater variation was required.

These curranty cakes seem to predominate on the western side of England – something to do, it has been suggested, with the arrival of dried fruit and spices mainly into the great port cities of Liverpool and Bristol.

A long way south of Manchester, and south also of those Coventry godcakes mentioned earlier, is to be found the Banbury cake, appealing because alongside currants and spices it contains citrus peel, and appealing also because I'd never been to Banbury and there were things there that I wanted to see.

Besides the cake, that is: primarily the constituent parts of the nursery rhyme, in so far as that was possible and legal and my memory of said rhyme allowed. I tried to recall it as I renewed my questing, by car this time, and trundled up the M40:

> *Ride a cock horse to Banbury Cross*
> *To see a fine lady upon a fine horse...*

Was that right? It didn't seem right; that repetition of horse was clumsy. What was the rest?

> *With rings on her fingers and bells on her toes*
> *She shall have... something... wherever she goes.*

And I shall have that rhyme running through my head wherever I go, I thought, turning off the motorway at the Banbury signpost and being funnelled without much fuss – or much choice – into an area dominated by car parks. Not very picturesque, and no sign of any horses, crosses or cakes.

However, there was a sign at the pedestrian exit from my chosen car park: Canal; Castle Quay Shopping Centre; Museum. The latter seemed promising.

It turned out to be terrific, at least for my slightly bizarre purposes.

One entered, slightly weirdly, via the shopping centre (newish, clean, mix of chain stores, vacant premises and cheapo sweet stalls). Up the steps to the museum, and the first thing I encountered was a cock horse, or what I would have called a hobby horse: a relatively realistic wooden horse's head stuck on the end of a pole with a pair of wheels at the other extremity. I patted it on the nose. One box ticked. Sort of.

In another corner was a broken stone cross: the original Banbury Cross, toppled by the Puritans! Since there was no one else around, I rapped the cross with a knuckle, you know, just to say that I had... and it was plastic. Ah well. Another box ticked. Sort of.

I took some notes in front of the cabinet dedicated to Banbury cakes, and then headed downstairs to the museum café, where I was sure that I would find the cakes themselves, because, if you were running a café in a museum in a town that had a cake named after it, you would serve said cake, wouldn't you? They do in Coventry, at a motor museum, after all.

But not in Banbury. Not much call for them, I was told. I made it out on to the market square. It was a sunny Saturday in November, and fake snow was blowing around from the Santa's Grotto scene set up by the local chamber of commerce. A wholesome adult female elf was doing her best to persuade toddlers and their parents that a word with Santa in his tent was a good idea; I didn't see any takers.

Market stallholders were doing a bustling pre-Christmas trade. The buildings around the edge of the market square were faced in glorious golden stone – this is the northern fringe of the Cotswolds – and if I half-closed my eyes and looked only at the roofs and what was above and behind them it was just possible to conjure a glimpse of life in the old town.

I was ducking down side streets at every opportunity and enquiring at every food outlet for my quarry. I was optimistic about Bishop's Bakes, but the lady behind the counter echoed the museum café line: no demand for Banbury cakes these days.

Halfway down Church Lane, little more than an alley, I struck lucky. There was a tremendously unpromising shop called Sugar Rush, sparsely stocked with luridly packaged snacks and looking like an unlikely offshoot of the American 'candy' stores that pop up all the time to besmirch London's West End.

But this one had a classy touch that none of those emporia will ever boast: a window display of cellophane-wrapped Banbury cakes – and a billboard on the alley boasting of their presence.

I was in there in a flash, and out again clutching three packs of three Banbury cakes – not tremendously artisanal but at least purchased in the correct town.

I had tried everywhere I could find to secure freshly made baked-on-the-premises-this-morning Banbury cakes, and asked everyone I met in the town who seemed likely to have a relevant view on the matter. To no avail. I had also sought out the Banbury cheese that historic sources had suggested was the ideal accompaniment to the cakes, again without success. This was no slur on the cheesemongers of the town, by the way – as far as I can ascertain, that cheese no longer exists.

Still, I had Banbury cakes that were made – consults label – er, on an industrial estate in Witney. Which is no more than forty minutes' drive from Banbury, via the M40, A34 and A40, so local. And I was about to eat them next to Banbury Cross, if I could find it.

The current Cross, a successor to the one pulled down by the Puritans and commemorated in ersatz form in the museum, sits in a flowerbed in the centre of a small traffic roundabout on the outskirts of the town centre. It is not very cross-like at all, but looks like a sort of Victorian space rocket, or the top half of a gothic revival steeple. One can't sit next to it, unless one sits in the middle of the aforementioned flower-bed, and in any case one would be constantly surrounded by circulating trade vans trying to make sense of the one-way system.

On the far side of the road, behind a steel safety barrier, is a fine lady on a fine horse, or at least a statue of same. I thought for one moment that the fine lady, who wears a toga and is riding side-saddle, might be waving a Banbury cake in her raised hand, but in fact she is just showing off the rings on her fingers (she also has bells on her toes).

There was no sign of a cock horse, but I had already seen one in the museum, so the omission was bearable.

There was a coffee house on the corner of West Bar Street and Horse Fair, overlooking the Cross and its roundabout. They didn't sell Banbury cakes – I knew they wouldn't – but I bought a cup of coffee and nobody objected when I opened up my pack of three cakes to sample them in sight of Cross, fine lady, fine horse, etc.

A Banbury cake does not differ greatly from an Eccles cake and its Lancashire cousins – they are all survivals of cakes served at medieval religious festivals, when a few currants counted as an exotic filling.

It was more elongated than its northern counterpart, resembling a small, plump, sugar-dusted pitta bread. But what really distinguished the Banbury cake was – I knew from studying the display in the museum – the spices and peel added to the currants, the former supposedly first brought back to the town by crusading knights in the thirteenth century. The cakes were first recorded in 1586, when they were being made in Parsons Street by one Edward Welchman. They became tremendously popular in the eighteenth century and were, the museum claims, 'exported to Australia, India and America', but they must have been pretty uninspiring by the time they got there, because mine had travelled about a quarter of a mile and weren't about to change anyone's life.

The spices were faintly detectable, along with preserved citrus peel, so that the Banbury cake most closely resembled a long and rather tired mince pie. I have no doubt that a shorter lifespan and a chunk of characterful cheese would have improved matters, but the whole experience had been frankly dispiriting.

If I could amalgamate the best components of my quest for the true slice of medieval religious festival cake – the rich goodness of the freshly made Eccles cake and the ancient charms of Banbury's marketplace – banish traffic noise and canned pop music, replace ersatz snow with the real stuff and add a sprinkling of holiday excitement… what a magical experience that would be, and how delicious and escapist those humble currranty pastries would seem.

But it all seemed a long way off as I trudged back through the marketplace towards the shopping centre and car park. At one stall a teenager with a bowler hat was selling Oreo Cookie cakes. Next door I was offered a Black Forest gâteau loaf, and a near-neighbour was touting Mars Bar batter cakes.

Enough. I shook the reins on my imaginary cock horse, and galloped out of town.

ECCLES CAKES

Felicity Cloake is one of my favourite food writers. Her weekly column in the Guardian *examines a different popular dish every week and provides a recipe which synthesises the best of many methods. That seems a sensible approach to take with an old-fashioned cake for which many families have preferred tweaks. This is Felicity's version.*

MAKES 10 ECCLES

For the pastry (or you can use 500g ready-made all-butter puff pastry)

250g strong white bread flour

5g fine salt

250g cold butter, cut into 2½ cm cubes

125ml cold water

For the filling

120g currants

50g mixed peel

zest and juice of ¼ lemon and ¼ orange

1 tbsp brandy, rum or whisky

50g butter, at room temperature

40g light muscovado sugar

½ tsp grated nutmeg

¼ tsp ground allspice

1 egg white

demerara sugar, to top

1. Stir together the currants, mixed peel and zest with the fruit juice and brandy, cover and set aside.
2. Mix the flour and salt together, then lightly rub in the butter until it's in small flakes (alternatively, pulse in a food processor). Gradually stir in about 100–120ml of cold water until you have a dough, but stop working the pastry as soon it comes together.
3. Roll out the pastry on a lightly floured surface into a rectangle three times as long as it is wide, trying to keep the edges fairly straight. Fold the top third down into the middle, then the bottom third up over the top, then rotate the pastry 90 degrees so the fold is now facing you. Roll out again and repeat, then wrap in clingfilm and chill for 20 minutes; then repeat the entire process, and chill for an hour.

4. Preheat the oven to 200°C/400°F/Gas Mark 6. Beat together the butter and sugar until well combined, then stir in the fruit and spices.

5. Roll the pastry out on a lightly floured work surface to about ½ cm thick, then cut out rounds about 9cm wide. Put a small teaspoon of filling in the centre of each, then dampen the edge of the circle and bring the edges into the middle, pressing together to seal. Put on a baking tray smooth side up, and squash slightly until flattened. Repeat with the rest, then brush with egg white and sprinkle with demerara sugar. Cut three slashes in the top of each and bake for about 20–25 minutes until golden and well-risen. Allow to cool slightly before tucking in.

CHAPTER 3
DUNDEE CAKE

I was looking forward to moving the story of cake along a bit. No disrespect to the Anglo-Saxon folk of Butser, nor the citizens of Eccles and Banbury, but their cakes had been somewhat basic, in keeping with their ancient status. Happily, there are cakes with a lengthy pedigree that are more substantial, and one of those was to be my next target.

At around the time that the less well-off people of these islands were happy to mark religious festivals with simple cakes of pastry and currants, the gentry celebrated special occasions with a 'Great Cake', a vast, dense fruit cake based on a mixture of flour, butter and ale and containing not just currants but other dried fruits from home and abroad, nuts, peel and exotic herbs and spices, all mixed with substantial quantities of expensive sugar before being baked and – if the occasion merited it and the budget allowed – decorated with marzipan.

Surviving recipes vary – the culinary chroniclers Sir Kenelm Digby and Hannah Glasse give examples from the seventeenth and eighteenth centuries respectively, and the concept will have changed little over hundreds of years – but the result will always have been rich, substantial and dense. Descendants of these hefty cakes are still common – they are merely disguised as our Simnel cakes at Easter and our Yuletide Christmas cakes, under layers of marzipan and icing. There is another celebrated British cake in this tradition, though, that is unadorned with decoration – except some nuts – and need not be consumed at a particular date on the calendar. It even has, as we shall see, a supposedly Tudor history of its own: Dundee cake.

It's not easy to work out why some towns and cities have cakes named after them and some don't. Clearly, it's not to do with the size, fame or notoriety of the city: there's no London cake, Glasgow cake or Cardiff cake. And it's not obviously to do with any great distinction on the part of the cake: as I've pointed out, there isn't a great deal of difference between an Eccles cake and a Banbury cake and neither of them, with all due respect, is likely to set the culinary world on fire, for all their rustic charm. It seems to me that the cakes named after places that are still reasonably well known now are mostly hangovers from the nineteenth century, when mass travel became a possibility and places started to celebrate the highlights of their local cuisine in order to attract more visitors.

That was certainly the case with Banbury and Eccles, but it doesn't explain the persistence in the public consciousness of Dundee cake, product of a city that in the nineteenth century had many reasons for global renown besides baked goods, and which still has a great deal going on today. The enduring fame of the city's cake may well be due in part to its commercialisation – complete with bogus historical back-story – at the height of the city's power, wealth and prestige, when tins of this tasty and easily portable product were sent far and wide as gestures of goodwill, and helped to lodge in the mind of a widespread audience not only the name of the city but the name of the cake.

There's no question that the fame of the cake endures: it's on display in a prime position in Harrods' Food Hall, and at Fortnum & Mason, accolades awarded only to foodstuffs of unquestioned clout, which guarantee wider awareness.

But it's also on sale in Marks & Spencer and Tesco, and a staple of the village bake sale. And unlike any other British cake, it is currently under consideration as a food name with Protected Geographical Indication (like Stilton cheese, Gloucester Old Spot pork and Cornish clotted cream), and has its own chunk of the British government's website to back this up.

We'll come back to the international legal status of the cake in a while. First of all, I had to get to Dundee to eat some.

'Why?' my wife, Ingrid, enquired. (I should just point out here that, technically, she's not my wife, but we've lived together for nearly thirty years and she hates the word 'part- ner.') 'You've already told me that you can get it down the road in M&S.'

I explained, not for the first time, the concept of my cake- quests and the need for authenticity of location for consumption, and Ingrid, not for the first time, rolled her eyes.

'Good luck,' she said, and I like to believe that she said it supportively. 'It's a long way.'

That's true. London to Dundee is not a journey for the faint-hearted, unless they run to air tickets, which I deemed excessively extravagant.

Rail, then, and even aboard trains which were for once obedient to their schedule, the trip took eight hours from my door to that of my hotel in Dundee.

Hotel! More extravagance. But justified, I felt. I had done some calculations while juggling railway timetables and maps of Dundee city centre, and while it was just about conceivable to travel from London to Dundee, eat cake in Dundee, and return to London on the same day, such an expedition would be fraught with risk. One delay due to leaves on the line, or one hiccup in the cake provision department and I'd be a chapter short.

So I felt that the hotel, a reasonably priced but not unstylish set-up in the centre of town, was justified for the additional peace of mind it provided – even though on arrival I was greeted in reception by half a dozen staff members in very fancy dress: Roman centurion, Viking warrior, Edwardian detective...

'Is it a theme night?' I asked the sensibly attired young lady behind the desk. 'Staff Christmas party,' she explained. 'So I'm afraid the bar is closed to guests tonight.'

It was 5 February.

Next morning, undisturbed, it must be said, by any staff-related shenanigans and well rested, I steamed off up the hill heading for Fisher & Donaldson, nominated by several

Dundee-savvy friends as the best spot for cake purchase and consumption.

It was two decades since I had last been to the fine city on the banks of the silvery Tay, and I was aware that big changes had taken place: new developments, museums, attractions and so on. So I WhatsApped friends who had more up-to-date knowledge and asked them what the best things to do were on arrival in Dundee.

Leave as soon as possible, one embittered individual suggested, but others were more generous, and all had agreed that Fisher & Donaldson was a sound choice for cake.

Dundee cake is a fruit cake topped with almonds, to put it simply. Or, to put it less simply, as in the documents submitted to government when applying for Protected Geographical Indication, 'a rich, moist, all-butter "afternoon tea" fruit cake which must be prepared, decorated and baked in the described geographical area'. That is, within the Cake Boundary as specified in the documents.

The early signs at Fisher & Donaldson were encouraging: Dundee cakes lined up in the window, large and small, done up in cellophane and tartan ribbon. I went inside.

There was a queue, which I joined at the wrong end, having misread the rope and bollard situation. I got in line behind half a dozen people buying morning rolls and loaves and reached the end of the queue only to be confronted by a hand-written sign which read 'Sorry, but the café section is closed today', the notice reinforced by a line of chairs blocking off the table area.

Blast. Thwarted.

'I'm sorry, but I was hoping to sit down with a slice of Dundee cake,' I said to the lady behind the counter, who had a bubbly perm and a fair bit of blue eyeliner.

She shook her head, making her ringlets dance. No way. Maybe if I had joined the right end of the queue.

It was disappointing. I might have purchased a slice and taken it out on to the street to consume, thereby eating Dundee cake in Dundee, job done; but I felt that it would be most appropriate to eat the cake on the premises of a cake shop – especially because F&D provided chairs and tables for this purpose, and it was clear that many Dundonians regularly indulged in this manner.

So I made my excuses and left.

This, I muttered to myself, is why a hotel was essential. Imagine if I had a train to catch in twenty minutes, I chuntered on, and a long trek across the city to fit in...

Feeling alternately cross and smug, and very cold, I turned left at the top of the street and proceeded in a westerly direction.

Fisher & Donaldson, my diligent research on the way up on the train had revealed, had another branch in the city, though it had not been entirely clear whether this also provided seating to cake consumers.

My path took me away from the city centre, which was characterised by wide thoroughfares, hefty Victorian edifices, kilt stores and bagpiping buskers, and into university territory, academic buildings of many ages and styles set back from the road, and all the ancillary services that the modern student requires in the shops on the Perth Road.

I walked past Kurdish barbers and edgy music stores, secondhand bookshops, organic cafés – and the fancy dress store which had no doubt outfitted the hotel staff the night before.

Just as I was starting to wonder if the Perth namechecked in the street signs might be Perth, Western Australia, the bright awning of Fisher & Donaldson's second city branch came into view. A man was cleaning the windows as I approached and swiped clear the suds to reveal a display dominated – as in the sister store – by Dundee cake.

A fearsome-looking fellow stood behind the counter as I entered the otherwise empty premises. He had the build of a caber-tosser and a red beard on a Victorian scale, but the tattoos on his partially shaven skull and the hefty nose-ring brought him bang up to date.

'What can I do for you?' he asked, and I expected him to add, 'Before I throw you in the Tay?'

I explained that what I really wanted, if it wasn't too much trouble, was one of their smaller Dundee cakes

'And I'd like to eat it here, if I may, with a nice cup of tea.' I indicated the little seating area at the back of the shop – just four tiny tables, each with a pair of chairs.

He raised his substantial eyebrows, then broke into a charming smile. 'No problem at all,' he said.

He brought over my cake, still wrapped in cellophane and tied with a twee double-knotted tartan ribbon, and my tea.

'That's the first time I've served Dundee cake for breakfast,' he noted. The menu on the table suggested that regulars more often opted for a bacon roll.

But I couldn't wait to get started. The cake was about the size of a cricket ball, but squidgier, and once I had got the ribbon undone (not without a lot of fiddling) I called for a knife and a plate and got down to some serious sampling.

I was utterly confident in both my cake and my location: the varied selection of Dundonians I had consulted, all born and bred or long-term residents, had all mentioned Fisher & Donaldson as purveyors of the real thing for near on a century. The royal warrant on their takeaway boxes was an additional mark of esteem. I was actually seated in one of their shops, in actual Dundee, within a clootie dumpling's throw of the actual silvery Tay.

A truer slice you could not wish to see – or eat. So I did. To bite into a hefty slice of Dundee cake is to be plunged into a world of fruity goodness, a mouthful crammed with concentrated, tangy sweetness, currants and sultanas bound in golden dough with the crunch of almonds for a textural counterpoint. It falls to bits when it meets the knife, as if previously held together by a mysterious force that the eater unleashes. If – as seems likely – this is the kind of thing that medieval cooks served up as a Great Cake, it is easy to see why it was such a highlight of the year.

The technique for eating it – the only possible technique for eating it – was to pick up as much as three fingertips and a thumb could encompass, compress, and insert the blob into the gob. How on earth the prim ladies of Dundee managed this at afternoon tea without scattering dried fruit all over their fitted carpets was beyond me.

The specification of the fruit is important – not only in the official documents, but in the unofficial history. Dundee cake – here comes that phrase so well-worn in British cake histories – 'according to legend', was first made for Mary, Queen of Scots in the sixteenth century. Mary was a formidable monarch who could take a tough line with her courtiers, and she is said to have made it clear that she couldn't abide cherries, which were apparently appearing too often for her liking in the cakes produced by the royal kitchens.

But a fruit cake without cherries was simply dull, and monarchs are often disinclined to accept dull, so some bright spark suggested replacing the cherries with almonds, and furthermore arranging the almonds in an attractive manner on the top of the cake.

The rest is history, or rather the rest is marketing bunkum invented in the nineteenth century and still peddled by otherwise respectable cake manufacturers to this day.

The true story, endorsed by many respectable sources and included in the PGI documents, is that Dundee cake was developed commercially in the nineteenth century by the Keiller family, who had a shop in the Seagate area of the city.

Janet Keiller established the family's fortune in the previous century when she perfected a revolutionary form of marmalade, spreadable rather than only cuttable in chunks, as had previously been the case. Her descendants expanded the business, using Seville oranges and other ingredients traded through Dundee's thriving international port.

Dundee cake, in which marmalade is an essential ingredient, imparting not only rich flavour but moisture and stickiness, was a diversification for the Keillers, something that their staff could make during the times of the year not dedicated to seasonal marmalade and preserve manufacture.

The almonds were nothing to do with Mary, Queen of Scots, but were traded through Spanish merchants, most likely associated with those who traded in the Seville oranges that were central to the Keillers' prosperity. Arranging the almonds in a pretty pattern on top of the cake made it distinctive in a way that the vital – but invisible – marmalade could not.

The reason that I wasn't consuming a Keiller's cake was that the family sold the business in the 1920s; it went through a series of owners and ceased to produce marmalade, cake or anything else for the UK market late last century.

In one sense, though, the family still provides comfort to the nation: Monty Don, the immeasurably reassuring presenter of the BBC's *Gardeners' World* programme, is a great-great-great-great-grandson of Janet Keiller.

'Are you OK there?' I had drifted off, wondering if Monty grew oranges, and my fulsomely bearded friend wanted to know if I fancied another cake.

I said I thought that one cake – even a modestly sized cake – was probably enough for breakfast, and he agreed.

It was a cold, crisp Monday morning and I felt that I had already overachieved for the day, if not the week, but I knew that I had to keep moving. Sitting down, even for a moment, would result in a post-cake coma.

I'm no good at walking aimlessly around a place. I need a mission, and I'd already ticked the box that I had come to Dundee to tick. What now?

Then I recalled that the museum in Banbury had proved unexpectedly informative on the topic of the town's cake, so I decided to see if the Dundee equivalent would be similarly forthcoming. The McManus would sort me out, I was sure. This museum occupies a splendid Victorian building – the work of Sir George Gilbert Scott – smack in the centre of town, next to the High School and over the road from the imposing DC Thomson HQ.

At the bottom of the street, a bagpiping busker serenaded at deafening volume a strappingly life-sized statue of Desperate Dan from *The Dandy*: an emphatically Dundonian spectacle.

I love a good old-school museum and the McManus was certainly that, crammed with fascinating items from the city's extraordinary past. But my needs were specific.

'Do you have anything about Dundee cake?' I asked the attendant at the entrance to the main galleries.

'There's cake in the café,' she said. 'Home-made carrot cake. With frosting.'

'No, no. I mean displays of cake. About cake. Cake-related items.'

'Well... not that I can recall. Have a look in The Making of Modern Dundee, though, on the ground floor here. There's a lot of stuff from old shops in there, maybe some cake too.'

Sounded good. I toddled off to the indicated gallery.

Everywhere I had turned for information about the city prior to this visit had told me that it had been celebrated for 'jam, jute and journalism'. The jam I understood – that was the Keillers and their competitors, bustling around over preserving pans stuffed with imported fruit to make Dundee the conserve capital of the world. The journalism was centred on DC Thomson, publishers of *The Beano* and *The Dandy* as well as many worthier titles for many years, and still an employer of many hacks in the city. But jute? Search me.

Thankfully, The Making of Modern Dundee enlightened me. If you're interested I can tell you that this is strong, natural fibre that is extracted from the bark of the jute plant, which is mainly found in India, Pakistan and Bangladesh – and which was imported in colossal quantities into Dundee in the nineteenth century, whereupon most of it was made into sacks.

And if you're really, really interested in jute, (a) you are probably reading the wrong book, and (b) there is an entire museum devoted to it in Dundee, called Verdant Works. Which I decided, having discovered as much as I felt I needed to know on the topic, not to visit.

But I digress. Inside the room, I had been hoping to find a display along the lines of Banbury's, with stacks of replica cakes, sacks of plastic almonds and plaster oranges, maybe an artist's impression of Mary, Queen of Scots Disdaining a Glacé Cherry. It was, for my specialised purposes, a disappointment. There were lots of old copies of *The Dandy*, a bottle of sperm oil from the whaling industry, and a stuffed pigeon called Winkie, who had won a medal for reporting an air crash. But nothing about cake except an empty tin, high in a glass case of items from a long-lost grocery store, that proclaimed its contents as 'Keiller's Dundee Cake – The Original' and displayed the royal warrant, ancestor of that now proudly displayed by Fisher & Donaldson.

I checked out the McManus's café, just to be sure, and they were indeed offering what looked like a mighty fine carrot cake. Dundee cake – that of Messrs Goodfellow & Steven – was available in the gift shop, in a trendy box, but at £10.95, I didn't feel it was a compelling purchase.

In any case I felt that having sampled Dundee's most traditional museum I should also have a look at a more recent establishment – the extraordinary branch of the Victoria & Albert Museum that has landed like a spaceship, or like a space-going version of a sailing ship, right on the waterfront by the Tay.

My hope was that the V&A, unlike the McManus but perhaps inspired by the memory of cake-fan Queen Victoria herself, might see the cultural value in a large and informative display about Dundee cake.

But no. Another tremendous museum, another almost total lack of Dundee cake. Admittedly the V&A's focus is Scottish design, and the Dundee cake can hardly be said to have been designed by anyone, being the result more of the evolution and democratisation of the ancient Great Cake than a single guiding vision.

But the museum did offer a remarkably preserved example of the tearoom, the British temple to the consumption of tea and cake that found its most elegant expression in Scotland, with the work of the renowned architect, furniture and interior designer Charles Rennie Mackintosh.

CAKE

Almost lost in the cavernous and ultra-modern interior of the museum sits a much cosier space: the entire preserved and conserved interior of the Oak Room from Miss Cranston's Ingram Street tearoom, one of a quartet of such premises owned by that redoubtable lady in Glasgow in the early twentieth century.

The tearoom emerged and prospered in the latter half of the nineteenth century, growing out of the widespread temperance movement that disparaged the consumption of alcohol, and the need for what we would now term 'safe spaces' in which increasingly emancipated women, freed from their own restrictive households, could meet and talk together.

Even when removed so completely from its bustling Glaswegian origin, the room is fascinating. Mackintosh's blue-accented wooden pillars lead the eye upwards to lattice lanterns that suffuse the space with a gentle light. It seems a place of calm and quiet, but then almost imperceptibly at first background noise seeps in, a soft recording of genteel chatter and the tinkle of teaspoon on china; discreet hubbub.

It's remarkably atmospheric, an effective tribute to the power of tea – and, yes, cake – to power social change.

Parked next door to the ship-shaped V&A is a real ship with an extraordinary history of its own and a connection – you won't be surprised to hear – with cake.

This is the RRS (Royal Research Ship) *Discovery*, built in Dundee, which took Robert Falcon Scott and his crew to

72

Antarctica in 1901, stayed there with them, locked in the ice, over two winters, and returned to British waters in 1904.

Discovery is an excellent preserved museum vessel now, with a modern educational and exploratory centre next door to her on the riverbank. None of these feature Dundee cake... but when, in 2016, archaeologists from the New Zealand-based Antarctic Heritage Trust were investigating Antarctica's oldest building – a hut on Cape Adare – they found a tin of fruit cake. The cake was wrapped in paper and still encased in the remains of a cake tin, and according to one of the team who found it, 'There was a very, very slight rancid butter smell to it, but other than that the cake looked and smelled edible.' The trust says that there is no doubt that the extreme cold helped to preserve the cake for all these years.

They concluded that the cake had almost certainly been brought from the UK by Robert Falcon Scott and his fellow explorers more than a century before, and had been preserved, almost intact if not quite edible, by the extreme cold.

There was evidence on the tin which proved – unfortunately, for my purposes – that the cake had been made by the English firm of Huntley & Palmers rather than Keiller's, but I like to think that the spirit of Dundee, as well as the goodness of rich fruit cake, travelled with Scott and his men aboard *Discovery*.

Some might say that Dundee cake provides more calorific value than interest, and it's true that it's neither the most aesthetically appealing nor flavourful creation to be found in this book. Some might go so far as to argue that its religious cousin, the Easter-related Simnel cake, in which the whole almonds are replaced by a layer of marzipan topped with marzipan balls representing the apostles, has much more going for it.

I accept that a Dundee cake bought in Marks & Spencer's in, say, Reading would serve little purpose except as an emergency standby for unexpected teatime visitors. But a Dundee cake made in Dundee, purchased in Dundee and eaten in Dundee has the whole city behind it.

And the city does not, in my experience, have much else of a culinary nature to recommend it. Fresh off my train on arrival and seeking a base layer for the following morning's cake-tasting, I dined out at Tony Macaroni's down by the Tay, and was startled by the scale of the pizza they served up – and more startled to be offered chips as an additional topping.

After that, the city's eponymous cake seemed a modest and appealing prospect, even at breakfast time. It's an honest cake, and a worthy representative of an energetic and friendly city. I understand the misgivings of some of my friends, who have seen scattergun developments defiling, as they see it, the Victorian face of the place. But I must say I loved it, and I wish the city and its bakers the very best of luck in trying to gain official recognition for the fact that their own cake can only come from their own place.

Work started more than ten years ago on what was initially intended to be an application for Protected Geographical Indication from the European Union, a process that is – at least for the foreseeable future, and for obvious reasons – redundant. The current PGI application was turned down recently by the British government, which claimed that the cake was 'generic'. The outraged bakers of Dundee are appealing.

In any case, all this bureaucracy seeks to define what a Dundee cake should be, and where it should come from, which will have the inevitable effect of preventing innovation or evolution – at least of anything that calls itself Dundee cake.

But it is typical of the city that there are new ideas that will not be stymied by any government's actions. Dundee cake gin, for example, enthusiastically recommended to me by a fancy-dressed member of my hotel's staff who was clearly well acquainted with it, Dundee cake chocolate (I have a bar beside me as I type), and Dundee cake ice cream, under development by Dundee College catering students, who are tapping into the great Italian-Scottish gelato traditions of families such as the Crollas and the Nardinis.

The flavourful flights of fancy are a tribute not only to the clout of Dundee cake as a brand, but to the staying power of substantial fruit cake as a concept. No medieval cook, stirring a vast pot of the mixture before it was baked, could have conceived of the journeys that such a cake would later fuel, or the exotic dishes and drinks that would later be based on it. The Great Cake had a great future.

DUNDEE CAKE

Many Dundonians have their own recipes for the city's famous cake, passed down through the generations and tweaked to allow for personal preferences and temperamental ovens. But this recipe has been agreed upon en masse by the trade organisation of Dundee's Master Bakers, who kindly shared it with me, and should settle any arguments.

MAKES ONE 18cm ROUND DUNDEE CAKE

250g slightly salted butter

250g caster sugar

5 eggs (250g), at room temperature, beaten

75g thick peel Seville orange concentrate (candied peel can be used instead or in addition, but the concentrate helps give a greater intensity of orange flavour)

finely grated zest of 1 orange

280g plain flour, sifted

450g sultanas

2 tbsp Amontillado sherry

50g whole blanched almonds, to top

DUNDEE CAKE

1. Preheat the oven to 180°C/350°F/Gas Mark 4. Line the cake tin and protect the outside with thick brown paper. Warm the butter and sugar.
2. Beat the sugar and butter until very light and creamy. Gradually beat in the eggs.
3. Fold in the orange concentrate, orange zest, flour and sultanas. Add the sherry and mix to a soft, dropping consistency. If it is too stiff, add a little milk.
4. Turn into the cake tin, level the top and cover with the whole almonds.
5. Bake for about 2½ hours, depending on the depth of the cake. If it starts to brown too much on the top, cover it with a sheet of foil.
6. When cool, wrap it in greaseproof paper and foil. To eat at its best, keep it for at least a week before using. The cake should keep for a month in an airtight container in a cool place. Do not refrigerate it.
7. When cutting traditional cake such as this Dundee cake, always use a long, sharp knife, preferably with a fluted edge, and use a sawing motion and the sharpness of the blade to cut the cake, not downward pressure which will cause it to crumble. Ideally, dip the blade into a jug of warm water, wiping the blade clear of excess water between cuts.

CHAPTER 4
QUEEN VICTORIA'S SANDWICH

The long railway journey home from Dundee allowed plenty of time to think about what my next cake objective should be. The Keillers and their fellow citizens had popularised something that had been a treat for the privileged few for hundreds of years, creating a cake both ancient and modern and allowing me to move the story along the centuries with one indulgent plateful.

But for all its sumptuous fruitiness and marketability, a Dundee cake is still old-fashioned and a long way from the pastel-coloured sponges and exotic fillings that today's hungry punters expect. My next cake should be a bridge between the old palace cookhouse and the contemporary kitchen, between primitive culinary techniques and industrial chemistry. And thinking on all this, as my train trundled southwards, I recalled the cake stalls of my boyhood... when I had visited many, many cake stalls.

Here's why. And I say this not to brag, but to explain.

When I was growing up, in the 1960s and 70s, my father was famous. Sort of. Not glamorous, movie-star, international jet-set famous, but instantly recognisable to every adult in Britain who had access to a television set. Perhaps ubiquitous would be a better term.

Richard Baker was the BBC's leading newsreader. In those days, decades before cable, satellite and digital, and long before phones, tablets and laptops, families gathered around their television sets every evening. There were only two channels, and Dad read the main news most evenings on the more popular of the two.

His burly, avuncular presence was the embodiment of reassurance, and he manifested for twenty minutes in half the nation's living rooms every weekday evening at either six or nine o'clock; sometimes both.

I think it can reasonably be said that he didn't unduly exploit his fame. Back then, BBC presenters were not supposed to have sponsorship deals, or appear in advertisements, or endorse products for gain; so he didn't.

But he did open fêtes. Dad opened a lot of fêtes.

'Why are we going to Godalming on your only proper day off?' my mother would ask as we all piled into the family Rover at noon on a Saturday.

'What has Sidcup done to deserve your presence?' she would ask.

'Letchworth? In this weather? To what purpose?'

It was a favour to the aunt of a colleague in the newsroom, or the uncle of someone he knew from university, or a friend of a chap he had met in the Garrick. Fête-opening was always unpaid, and it was rarely local. And it was often quite fun, as long as we didn't get lost or traffic-jammed en route, because my father had a horror of being late for anything.

On arrival at the fête location, usually a municipal park or school sports field, Dad would ascend a platform, or perch on a hay bale, flanked perhaps by the beaming mayor and a simpering local beauty queen, and make a brief, self-effacing speech which he would adapt minimally for the needs of each neighbourhood ('I asked the BBC weatherman to arrange blue skies in Bognor today...') and which always featured the same anecdotes.

Then he would declare the proceedings open, and the family would embark on a kind of royal progress around the stalls, sideshows and attractions. It was fun to be fêted, and my brother and I were usually fussed over and treated in a highly satisfactory manner.

But we had to be careful not to win anything, since we would be obliged to give it back. This sense of *noblesse oblige* was reinforced by the occasion, often recalled with only slightly bitter amusement by my mother, on which my father, drawing a grand charity raffle, had pulled his own ticket out of the hat and won a house – a holiday chalet on the east coast, but still, an actual *house* – and felt immediately and correctly compelled, for decency's sake, to auction it off to raise further funds for the evening's cause.

So we were deliberately hopeless at heaving the welly, hoopla and beat the goalie, safe in the knowledge that our recompense would come at the cake stall, where Dad would be nobly obliged to buy something – and we wouldn't have to give it back.

The ladies of the Women's Institute, lined up in their best summer frocks behind the ranks of bakes, would flutter and trill at the approach of the handsome newsreader and his two blond little sons. Free samples of Margery's malt loaf or Mabel's ginger slab would be pressed upon us but no, my father would insist with a twinkle, he would certainly pay, and the boys must choose which slice they wanted...

James and I looked, at this stage in our lives, misleadingly like little angels, with golden hair, blue eyes and identical outfits. We were the same height, despite the fact that I was almost two years older and had to deny repeatedly that we were twins. I did this with a smile, despite my inner fury, because we were on duty and basking in the glow of reflected celebrity.

We played up to Dad's charm, cooing obediently over the choice of cakes and pretending to have some difficulty in making our selections as the matrons fluttered around us. But there was never any contest.

To our youthful and unadventurous palates, Victoria sandwich was the ideal between-meals treat, all the more so if the two halves were separated by cream as well as raspberry jam.

I cannot say that I experience a madeleine moment whenever I bite into a Victoria sandwich now – there were too many fêtes, and too many VS treats – but I'm aware that I go about eating this cake in the same way today that I did all those decades ago, juggling the slice to try to ensure that each mouthful contains not just cake but a bit of jam and (if it's there) cream.

And whenever I see a Victoria sandwich, sitting proudly uncut on a plate, I feel a tiny frisson of excitement, as ancient synapses are triggered and old hungers are reawakened. Reach out for it, my childhood self seems to be saying: it's not a feast for all the senses, but it may be all you get before suppertime.

Half a century later, a little bafflingly, given the rising tide of buttercream and the clamour for cupcakes, the Victoria sandwich retains its place of honour at such local festivities.

That's why it's the perfect cake to bridge the great divide between the simple curranty festival cakes of olden tymes, and today's garish extravagances. In its ubiquity at the church fête, the village gathering and the charity bazaar, it represents a link to the traditional role of the cake on saints' days, as in Eccles and Banbury. Yet the Victoria sandwich is clearly related – in the role, as it were, of Mother of the Empire – to the spectacular Showstoppers of the televised *Bake Off*.

Three years ago my friend Boo moved with her partner Harry from London to a lovely village in Dorset, where they have thrown themselves with gusto into local life. At the recent village show, Boo entered a number of produce categories, submitting A Vegetable Carved to Resemble an Animal, A Dozen Roses, and Three Courgettes with Their Flowers Attached, while the less green-fingered Harry entered a limerick in the poetry class and – with some bravery, I'd say – the Home Baking category, in which contestants were required to submit a Victoria sandwich.

It's interesting that the room for creative manoeuvre is so limited on these occasions. Just as the gardeners are limited to a specific number of examples of specific flowers and vegetables, so the bakers are enjoined to ignore whatever flights of autobiographical fancy they may have witnessed recently on *Bake Off* and instead to stick rigidly to the classic recipe.

'I've thought about this,' Boo said when I raised the matter with her, 'and I reckon it's to make the judges' lives a bit easier. It means they don't have to try and rank their friends and neighbours for artistic excellence, just work out how closely they have stuck to the recipe. Mind you, there will still be a row when the result is revealed.'

Harry got second prize for his limerick, but his Victoria sandwich was unplaced – because, Boo explained, instead of sprinkling the top of his cake evenly with icing sugar in the classic manner, he went completely mad and used a template to outline the initial letter of the name of the village in sugar instead.

'Rookie error,' Boo pronounced. 'He won't do that again.'

The True Slice of Victoria sandwich, then, must be by definition unexciting, conformist, well-behaved. According to Mary Gwynn, the author of *The WI Cookbook*, it should be: 'Buttery and light, filled with a layer of raspberry jam and with its golden surface dusted with a fine coating of caster sugar.' Gwynn also points out that 'Its very simplicity denotes the challenge it presents to bakers.'

Simple, but challenging; modest, but important. It's a cake that deserves special attention.

It also seems likely that the simplicity of this cake, its modesty and lack of extravagant decoration, exotic flavours or decadent fillings, were crucial in its appeal to the individual after whom it is named: Queen Victoria.

In his essay 'The Queen and Her Cakes', Michael Hunter, the curator of Victoria's home on the Isle of Wight, Osborne House, has suggested that the chief appeal of the cake which would come to be known as the Victoria sandwich was not the presence of deliciousness, but the absence of danger.

In the first half of the nineteenth century, Hunter explains, afternoon tea was served with seed cake and fruit cake, and it was believed that both seeds and dried fruits might be dangerous for small princes and princesses, presumably as they represented choking hazards.

Sponge cake, however, presented no such hazards and was thus ideal for inclusion among the tea-time treats on the table at Osborne House – the place above all others where Victoria could feel safest with her children around her, and the place where I felt I must go to find the True Slice of Victoria sandwich.

CRUMBS OF KNOWLEDGE
SPONGE

The terms 'Victoria sponge' and 'Victoria sandwich' are pretty much interchangeable: a pedant will point out that the item is properly called a sandwich because it sandwiches a layer of jam – most often jam and whipped cream, or jam and buttercream, in these decadent times – between two layers of a horizontally halved sponge cake.

In the annals of cake history, sponge comes along later than the great fruit cakes, which rise – in so far as they rise at all – through the lifting power of yeast, while sponge is lifted through the expansion of air as it heats in bubbles of beaten egg.

We don't have an exact date for the invention of sponge, but common sense suggests that it was likely to have coincided with the widespread adoption of implements suitable for the beating of eggs... and the fork did not catch on in Europe until the later Middle Ages.

So rather than 'invented', it might be better to say that the sponge cake evolved in Europe in the Middle Ages. While the Court of Savoy are undoubtedly the inventors of the sponge finger, the Spanish also lay claim to the earliest formulation of sponge cakes by manual means. But it was first recorded in the work of the Italian Renaissance chef Bartolomeo Scappi, while the English poet and chronicler Gervase Markham set down the first recipe for something that we would recognise as a sponge cake in 1615, though without calling it that.

At this stage the cakes – containing no fat, but simply eggs, flour and sugar – were probably still fairly dense and biscuity, at best like a sponge finger or a madeleine. For the next couple of centuries the quality of sponge relied almost entirely on the heft and stamina of the cook doing the beating, a good hour with fork and bowl being recommended for a satisfactory rise in a substantial cake.

The origins of the name are similarly obscure, though it may well have arisen through a pre-fork method of getting bubbles into egg whites, by squeezing them through a (natural, harvested from the sea) sponge. The earliest citation for the word in a cake context in the *Oxford English Dictionary* comes from a letter by Jane Austen to her sister Cassandra of 17 June, 1808, in which the novelist declares: 'You know how interesting the purchase of a sponge-cake is to me!'

The breakthrough into fluffy lightness on which the modern Victoria sandwich and other sponge cakes depend was down to the innovations of Alfred Bird, of whom more on page 95.

There might have been easier options for me. I could have simply gone to one of many places named after or associated with Queen Victoria and located a slice of Victoria sandwich. Most cities and a good many towns in the United Kingdom, as well as dozens in her former empire, would have provided a possible location, and while the sandwich is not as ubiquitous as once it was, an approximation of it can be found in countless tearooms.

For instance, I have worked for many years in an office above Victoria Station, on Victoria Street in the district of London called Victoria, an area liberally sprinkled with cake-equipped hotels, refreshment parlours and supermarkets. Job done!

But it wouldn't have felt right.

The True Slice needs to be an authentic example of the cake, served in a place not only relevant to the story of that cake, but resonant with associations. So not just a version of Queen Victoria's cake in a place named after her: a proper Victoria sandwich in a house built for her, where she lived and loved, and died.

My journey was similar to that often taken by the Queen Empress and her family and supporting retinue: by train from London and then by boat across the Solent to the Isle of Wight.

It was a journey that the monarch made several times every year from the palace's completion, in 1851, to her death exactly fifty years later. Osborne House is the most perfect expression of Victorian values, having been conceived and built entirely according to the wishes of Victoria and her consort, Prince Albert. And it is preserved as they lived there, since no other family than theirs was ever in prolonged residence.

I visited on a bright, early-summer day in a post-pandemic lull. There were few other visitors and many of the blinds were drawn to protect furniture and artworks from the sunlight; masked English Heritage volunteers stood sentry in the corners, and in the gilt and gloom of the corridors and state rooms, silence reigned.

This was not the scene of cheerful cake consumption, but I had done my homework and I knew where to go to find it.

Leaving the main house and crossing the elegant parterre, with its tulip beds and spectacular views across the Solent, I descended flights of steps and struck out along a single-track roadway through the estate and towards the coast.

Vast rhododendrons flanked the path, and there was birdsong and butterflies in the air; not a peep of the twenty-first century intruded.

Ten minutes' walk brought me to the gates of an extraordinary enclave within the grounds: the Swiss Cottage, built by Victoria and Albert for the education and enjoyment of their children.

This is surely the most unusual royal house in all the kingdom: a simple alpine chalet, built of pine wood in the classic Swiss style, with two main rooms on the first floor surrounded by a balcony and surmounted by a steeply pitched roof, and on the ground floor a kitchen, scullery and ancillary chambers.

All around the little house are kitchen gardens, laid out with beds of healthy vegetables and staked bushes that will bear summer fruits, and there are bright primroses on the verges.

I climbed the exterior stairs to the first floor, and walked gently into the sitting room, to find myself all alone with the ghost of Prince Albert's last tea party.

It was a plain little room, with monochrome family portraits hanging on the vanilla-painted walls and the space dominated by an oval table, set, an information card explained, as it was for tea on July 12 1861, the last occasion on which the whole family was together at Osborne before Prince Albert's death.

The Queen had recorded the occasion in her diary: 'Walked over to the Swiss Cottage... where I met Albert... & *all* the children & where the results of the morning's cooking were displayed and relished. We all sat down to tea...' I saw that eleven places were laid, each with a cushionless wooden chair, and flanking a modest arrangement of wildflowers at the centre of table were plates of sandwiches, sausage rolls and – thank goodness! – cake, including a large oblong slice of what was unmistakably Victoria sandwich.

Also unmistakably, it was made of plastic and on public display, so I wasn't about to eat it. But that spookily frozen tea party had given me the context for cake consumption at Osborne, and I knew where to go to complete the experience.

Urgent emails to English Heritage HQ – some of the battiest they had received for a while, no doubt – had established that the café at Osborne House would be open on the day of my visit, and that it was their custom to serve a variety of freshly made cakes, including Victoria sandwich.

But would there be any left?

There was. It was barely noon, and the nice lady behind the counter in the Orangery tearoom reassured me that, although she had already served several slices of Osborne Victoria Sponge – that's what they called it – ample supplies remained.

I asked for two slices, and a cup of tea, and took a seat close to one of the tall windows overlooking the terrace and the distant Solent. The sun shone on the elegant tulips as visitors picked their way among the formal beds, and in the Orangery there was a murmur of voices and the timeless tinkle of teaspoon on saucer.

I contemplated my two substantial slabs of VS, and became aware that two ladies in their seventies at a nearby table were contemplating me. Surely, they were thinking, he's not going to eat both of those all by himself?

I raised my spoon in greeting. 'Research,' I explained. And tucked in.

The cake was not quite authentic in Victorian terms: the colour – pale gold – and texture – quite firm and dry, almost crumbly – were fine, but as well as raspberry jam in the centre there was a slender layer of cream, whipped and subsequently firmed up in the fridge, which the monarch's children would no doubt have enjoyed, and which many of us know to be an essential element of today's Victoria sandwiches, but which was not included in the original conception of the cake.

The primary purpose of this cake, revolutionary in its day, was to liven up the standard slab of sponge in a simple yet delicious manner.

Nobody knows who first had the revelation that, instead of mixing flavourings into the body of a sponge cake, one could simply sandwich them between two entire cakes, but the elegance of the solution is such that it seems eternal.

One of the first appearances of the Victoria sandwich as such is in the ultimate compendium of English domestic life, *Mrs Beeton's Book of Household Management*, first published in 1861. A weird thing about the entry is that it doesn't appear in the Cake section – though there is a fat-free sponge cake there – but instead in the chapter headed Creams, Jellies,

Omelets etc. Another weird thing is that Isabella Beeton recommends baking the batter in a Yorkshire pudding tin rather than a cake tin... all of which suggests that she had in mind something that would be cut into fingers as a dessert rather than served in singular triumph as a cake.

But the essential ingredients and ratio of the Victoria sandwich are all there: the same weight of eggs, flour, sugar and butter; and some jam for the filling. The difference between a Victorian Victoria sandwich recipe and that used to make the cake I was eating at Osborne (see the English Heritage recipe below) is subtle but significant: Mrs Beeton – and no doubt Queen Victoria's cooks – used plain flour. Today's cook uses self-raising flour.

As any competent baker will know, the distinction is vital. The Victorian cake relied on eggs, and the beating heft of the cook's forearm, for its lift, while the modern cook has the invaluable assistance of the baking powder, which, with a hint of salt, is all that distinguishes self-raising flour from the plain variety.

The 'sponge' used in a Victoria sandwich is not a true or pure sponge, because it incorporates fat, in the form of the butter that is beaten with sugar ('creamed') before the addition of flour and eggs. This makes for a more rich, moist mixture than the pure sponge, and the greater lift and aeration crucial to the appeal of the Victoria sandwich is possible through the use of baking powder, initially added separately to the mixture but these days most often employed in the form of self-raising flour.

Cooks at Osborne in Queen Victoria's time would have filled the earliest versions of the sandwich with raspberry or strawberry jam made with fruit from the gardens – perhaps berries gathered from bushes in the Swiss Cottage plots. No doubt, given concern for the health and safety of the inmates of the royal nursery, the fruit would first have been pressed through a sieve with the back of a wooden spoon to remove any potentially lethal pips. And cream in the nineteenth century was regarded as a wholesome treat rather than a dietary danger.

CRUMBS OF KNOWLEDGE
MR BIRD'S BAKING POWDER

Alfred Bird (1811–78), whom we met briefly in Chapter One, was a Birmingham chemist and industrialist who became a hero of modern baking, driven by his passion for experimentation – and concern for his wife's delicate digestion.

Mrs Bird – Elizabeth – suffered from yeast intolerance and an allergy to eggs, which caused great misery and drove her husband to experiment with food chemistry in the family chemist's shop in the evenings.

He searched for a way of raising baked goods without employing yeast, and eventually, in 1843, came up with his baking powder, which worked by releasing bubbles of carbon dioxide when the mixture of bicarbonate of soda and tartaric acid was dampened. The basic chemistry had been known for centuries: Bird's genius lay in mixing the reactive ingredients with a starch to keep them dry and inert until mixed with liquid. This in turn allowed them to be mixed with flour to create the self-raising flour that takes so much work out of baking for the cook.

Bird did not patent his invention, which meant that others could innovate and profit by it, but he did well from supplying baking powder to the British troops fighting in the Crimean War. And he and his family would make millions, and acquire a fleet of yellow Rolls-Royces, from his innovation to deal with his wife's other digestive ailment – egg-free custard powder.

The latter was not only a great invention but a marketing triumph for the Birds, whose business mantra hung on the wall of their Birmingham premises: 'Early to Bed, Early to Rise. Stick to your Work – and Advertise.'

Alfred was a fascinating, polymathic character with tremendous silver mutton-chop whiskers, who, when not busy changing the course of culinary history in his laboratory, would entertain his friends by playing on a beautiful set of harmonised glass bowls, constructed to his specifications, whose notes extended over five octaves.

All of this ran through my mind as I consumed my cake in Osborne's Orangery. I had bought two slices because... well, because of unrestrained greed, but also because I somehow felt that I should match the amount of thinking that I needed to do about the substance with the quantity of it that I consumed. Not a good plan.

The fact is that a little Victoria sandwich goes a long way. This is a cake that is perhaps more valuable as a barometer of baking skill than as a treat in its own right.

This is why it is so often set as a test of a baker's competence – not only on *The Great British Bake Off*, but at all those country fairs, village celebrations and Women's Institute competitions, where the ingredients allowed are often carefully specified.

The Victoria sandwich cakes produced under these circumstances are not exercises in creative imagination, but tests of skill: how well do their bakers know their basic baking techniques? And how well, crucially, do they know their ovens?

But there is one more element that any cake, especially, perhaps, one as simple as the Victoria sandwich, demands: the magical, mystical gift of the true baker, the instinctive ability to know when heat and chemistry have combined to the optimum effect.

That gift, or the lack thereof, is the difference between baking genius and baking hack, between a baker who can follow a recipe and a baker who can invest the result of the recipe with magic.

My goodness. I'd finished both slices while my mind wandered.

Amazing, the inspirational power of a slab of cake. Well, two slabs. The seventy-something duo at the nearby table glanced my way, then whispered to each other. They may well have been wondering if I was about to go back for a third slice.

No ladies. No more cake.

Not that day, at least...

OSBORNE HOUSE VICTORIA SANDWICH

This recipe, from English Heritage, is fairly classical. If you feel the urge you can go completely crazy and use a different kind of cream or jam – or both! – but before you do I ask you to pause and consider: would Queen Victoria have approved?

SERVES 8

For the sponges
240g unsalted butter, softened, plus extra for greasing the tins

240g caster sugar, plus extra to dust the cake

4 eggs, lightly beaten

3–4 tbsp milk

2 tsp vanilla extract

240g self-raising flour, sifted

For the filling
200ml double cream

2 tbsp icing sugar

5 tbsp raspberry jam

QUEEN VICTORIA'S SANDWICH

1. Preheat the oven to 180°C/350°F/Gas Mark 4. Grease and line the bases of 2 x 20cm sandwich tins.

2. Cream the butter and sugar together until pale and fluffy, then add the beaten egg a little at a time, beating it into the mixture until it is all incorporated.

3. Add the milk and stir in the vanilla extract, then fold in the flour gently. Divide the mix between the two tins and level off using a spatula or palette knife.

4. Bake the cakes in the oven for around 25 minutes, or until a skewer inserted in the centre of each comes out clean.

5. Remove the cakes from the oven and rest them in the tins for 5 minutes. Remove the sponges from the tins, peel away the lining paper and place the sponges on a wire rack to cool.

6. Whisk the double cream with the icing sugar until soft peaks form. Sandwich the jam and cream between the two cooled sponges, sprinkle with caster sugar and enjoy.

CHAPTER 5
BATTENBERG CAKE

Half Moon Street is an elegant thoroughfare that runs straight from the heart of Mayfair to a junction with Piccadilly at the fringe of Green Park. There are no blowsy boutiques or vulgar brasseries, and nothing as showy as an Aston Martin or Bentley dealership: just two substantial but discreet hotels, one on each side of the road, and brass plates at Georgian doorways that hint at wealth management and private banking.

But I was not there to seek financial advice. Eccles and Dundee had shown me what mankind could do with dried fruit and inspiration. The Victoria sandwich at Osborne House had shown me the staying power of simplicity. Now I needed to find a cake with a bit of style and flamboyance about it, to head out of the nursery and into the world of style and sophistication. A cake conceived in the nineteenth century that thrived in the twentieth. And having headed to the far north and the deep south, I could achieve this objective not far from home, in central London.

CAKE

At the southern end of Half Moon Street is a vast hole in the ground, surrounded on three sides by the towering, scaffold-clad facades of a Victorian building. This is all that remains of the Naval & Military Club, known, after the traffic directions painted on its gateposts, as 'The In and Out' and a bastion of the British establishment for more than a century.

In a room at an annexe of the club at 42 Half Moon Street, on an autumn day in 1921, almost exactly 100 years before my mission, the first Marquess of Milford Haven drew his final, laboured breath.

He was sixty-seven years old and had been suffering from heart trouble following influenza. He was also under financial pressure. But in his time the Marquess – Louis – had been rich, and powerful, and royal: an Illustrious, Serene Highness, married into the most powerful royal family in the world, and as First Sea Lord the master of the Royal Navy, at the time the planet's most feared.

All that Louis – born Count Louis of Battenberg – is remembered for now is a cake.

But what a cake! Battenberg is a splendid creation: four squares of sponge in two contrasting colours, all surrounded by a layer of jam and an outer armour of marzipan. A slice looks wonderful on the plate, like a pastel-hued heraldic shield, and the contrast in textures and flavours in a single spoonful can be entrancing.

It is one of my most favourite cakes, and many share my view: it often features in the top five when British tastes in cake are surveyed. Just thinking about it on Half Moon Street made me long for a slice there and then.

My plan – call me a nut, or a crazy dreamer – had been to think over the strange story of Prince Louis, and the convoluted evolution of the cake that he inspired, over a slice or two of Battenberg cake in the street where he passed away. All the better if this could be done in the kind of surroundings that Louis, in his prime, would have recognised: luxurious and well populated with waiting staff, yet without incurring plutocratic levels of expenditure.

I had a powerful conviction that this fine cake surely survived in its original form somewhere close to the heartland of its inspiration. And I saw my quest to find it as a modest kind of public service, a way of putting a marker down and saying: Here, at this spot, one may, in the correct manner, enjoy an honest slice of proper Battenberg. Onwards!

Actually, it was a doddle. I asked one or two of my hungriest friends where I could get a decent slice of Battenberg in the neighbourhood of Piccadilly, and the consensus was... on Piccadilly, at the Wolseley, of course. I booked a table (not without a little to-ing and fro-ing, for the Wolseley is *always* busy) for mid-afternoon.

This former car showroom, 200 metres east of Half Moon Street, has a fair claim to being London's smartest restaurant, a pitch-perfect grand café created by Chris Corbin and Jeremy King and much beloved by movers, shakers and taste-makers.

I can hardly present the Wolseley as a discovery or a hidden gem, but it was a surprise and a useful revelation to discover that one can, at shortish notice, command a table here in mid-afternoon, order a slice of cake and a cup of tea, and enjoy just that – for little more than the price of a Big Mac and fries.

Of course, a certain resolve is required – not least to get past the uniformed doorman – and you will have to be steely to refuse when your charming waiter suggests the Classic Afternoon Tea at £33. But it can be done. Summon your inner Prince Louis, stiffen the spine, and say: 'I would like a slice of Battenberg cake, please, and a pot of Earl Grey.'

(Other teas are available. But this is the most suitable, I feel).

That is what I did. The slice of Battenberg was individually priced on the Wolseley's magnificent menu, at £5.75. And it was very fine.

Two quadrants of sponge were natural gold, two a pale green. I cut a green corner from my slice and lifted it to my lips, where a hint of pistachio blended with a trace of almond from the marzipan shell. This was coloured... orange... but I understood why when I bit into the cake, and the hint of apricot jam – a narrow seam, separating sponges, cake and shell – cut through the gentle sweetness.

This was not quite the traditional Battenberg of the vicarage tea party. But one could hardly carp at the substitution of subtly flavoured pistachio for food-colouring pink, nor the hint of apricot rather than raspberry jam. The flavours of the main constituents were individually present, and also worked in harmony. A Battenberg for the twenty-first century, nodding respectfully at its forebears and yet confidently self-assertive.

Not unlike the immaculately suited – and immaculately polite – Mr King, who shimmered over to enquire if all was well. It was.

I chewed, savoured, sipped my tea, and looked over the heads of my fellow customers and out through the great windows, down Piccadilly towards Half Moon Street, and considered where the Battenberg story began.

The story of Battenberg cake brings together not only the crowned heads of the noble families of Europe but also global conflict, philosophy, police cars and the Cedars of Lebanon.

I had considered travelling to the town of Battenberg itself, population 5,000 or so, in the Waldeck-Frankenberg district of the state of Hesse in Germany... This little settlement in the forested hills above the river Eder is, as far as can reasonably be established, the source of the family that is the inspiration for the cake's name. But there is little local evidence of pride about this.

These were testing times and it would not have been easy to simply jump on a plane to Germany on what seemed likely to be a wild cake chase, so instead I had combed the websites of the town's few modest hotels and restaurants, and in particular the two bakeries: Bakery Wack and the Bäckerei Michael Bienhaus.

At these you can clearly buy Battenberger Brötchen, little bread rolls, and Battenberger Landbrot, a cottage loaf, and a limited array of sweeter confections, heavy with imported fruit and whipped dairy goo. None of our targeted treat, though. I had emailed both bakeries, having fiddled around a bit with

Google Translate. 'Can a man,' I enquired in my best German, 'In Battenberg town visiting, Battenberg cake purchase?'

From Michael Bienhaus I heard nothing – he may still be puzzling over the grammar – but the Bakery Wack emailed back: 'Nein.'

It is hard to blame the bakers of Battenberg for their indifference. The cake, after all, is a strange memorial to their lost influence, a lasting reminder that the name of their town was adopted by the high and mighty to add the heft of heritage – and was then dropped when that heritage became diplomatically inconvenient.

The annals of the German aristocracy are vast and complex. The physical form of their pedigree handbook, the *Almanach de Gotha*, makes its English equivalent, *Debrett's*, look like a pocket diary. But I plunged in and hacked through the undergrowth of the Vons and Zus to discover the earliest instance of Battenberg in an aristocratic context, when a branch of the noble family of Wittgenstein (the same family whose name would be adopted by the ancestors of the great philosopher Ludwig Wittgenstein) started to call themselves the Counts of Battenberg in the early thirteenth century.

Curious to think that a name now forever associated with the highest intellectual analysis of logic, mathematics and metaphysics should also be associated with cake... but that line of Battenbergs died out in the fourteenth century, and the title was left lying around in the capacious lumber room of German nobility until, half a millennium later, it was picked up again, given an upgrade and a polish, and set on the path to brief global fame – and cake-based immortality.

This is where our man comes in. In the mid-nineteenth century, Prince Alexander von Hessen-Darmstadt, the brother of the Grand Duke of Hesse (who was very grand indeed), married Julia von Hauke, the orphaned daughter of the former Deputy Minister of War of Congress Poland. Their liaison was not considered befitting of his rank. You can almost hear the Hesses hissing: '*Poland...?*'

To even things up, Julia's brother-in-law had a look among the unemployed titles lying around the place, and created her Countess of Battenberg in 1851, with a further elevation to Princess of Battenberg in 1858. Her husband, who knew a good thing when he saw it, agreed to carry the same title and name, and another Battenberg dynasty was founded.

Alexander and Julia's son Ludwig is the man the cake is named after, although his own name would undergo multiple modifications during his lifetime.

I reached for another forkful of marzipan and sponge and considered the life and career of Ludwig, later Louis, late of Half Moon Street.

He was born Ludwig Alexander, His Illustrious Highness the Count von Battenberg, in Graz in Austria in 1854, and brought up in Italy and Germany. With his mother's promotion to Princess (thanks to her brother-in-law, the Grand Duke of Hesse, who could hand these titles out like sweets), he became His Serene Highness Prince Louis of Battenberg.

This made it easier for the young man to mingle on equal terms with his cousins and other relatives in the assorted royal houses of Europe. He became particularly fond of his cousins by marriage in the royal family of England, and as a teenager he became a British subject and joined the Royal Navy as a cadet. It is unclear at which point Ludwig was heavily modified into Louis, and why. But it would prove a handy adaptation.

Louis's admittance to a naval career was not entirely straightforward: he was medically unfit on account of his wheezy chest, feeble vision and slight curvature of the spine. But if he did not have the usual physical attributes of a naval officer, he unquestionably had friends in high places, and was allowed to join up without a medical certificate in order not to disappoint the Queen.

It was the making of him. From time to time the royal family would continue to intervene in Louis's career, for instance by expressing disappointment at the Admiralty's slowness in promoting officers who were also Princes, and with such aid – and his own undoubted determination and ability – he climbed through the ranks to become, eventually, First Sea Lord, not only the ceremonial head of the Royal Navy but also its chief of operations. At a time when Britannia still ruled the waves, Louis Battenberg ruled her Navy.

None of which has anything to do with cake. That connection was entirely to do with his marriage. To rewind a bit, in 1883 Queen Victoria appointed the good-looking, nattily bearded and impeccably royal young officer to the crew of her yacht, *Victoria and Albert*, and on 30 April, at Darmstadt, in the presence of the Queen, Louis married her granddaughter, Princess Victoria of Hesse and by Rhine.

The Hesse bit of her name indicates that she descended from Louis's family: the two were first cousins once removed, and had known each other since childhood. It might seem a bit weird, but it was the way of things in such circles until very recently. Queen Elizabeth II and her husband Prince Philip were cousins (and, of course, both related to our Louis).

The Battenberg cake, multiple recipe books and countless other sources claim, was invented in honour of the bridegroom at the time of the wedding. This certainly seems to be the only plausible explanation for the name of the cake, although actual evidence of the connection is hard to come by, and other suggestions linking the design of the cake to Louis' family seem to have been invented. At any rate, it explains why this very British cake has such a very Germanic name.

But just as his naval career peaked in the early years of the twentieth century, so it became something of a handicap for a senior British naval officer – and indeed for any member of the British royal family – to have an obviously German name.

With the country actually at war with Germany, it was decided that the Battenbergs in Britain should become something more – how should one put it, your Highness? – more *English*-sounding. Battenhill was considered, but in the end Louis settled on Mountbatten, and the royal family remain Mountbatten-Windsors to this day.

So Louis's name changed again, and he later added a knighthood to become Sir Louis Mountbatten in July 1917, before a final elevation, this time to the English peerage as The Most Honourable The Marquess of Milford Haven later that year.

Unfortunately his fortunes did not keep pace with his rank. At the outbreak of war he had to step down from his high rank in the Navy because of anti-German sentiment. He declined a dukedom because he could not afford the lifestyle which would accompany such a title; indeed, in 1919 he had to give up his family home, Kent House, for financial reasons. He also had to sell his treasured collection of naval medals, about which he had written three books.

All his investments in Russia were seized by rampaging Bolsheviks, and his German assets were decimated by the postwar collapse of the Deutschmark. He sold the family's German castle the year before his death.

So by the time he got to the room in the club annexe at 42 Half Moon Street he was in drastically reduced circumstances, having lost his name, his occupation and the vast majority of his fortune. His death was front-page news, not only in the English newspapers but in the *New York Times*, but he soon faded from the public imagination. His sweet memorial, however, persists.

But despite its popularity, the Battenberg is not without its detractors. For all the beauty and expertise of the Wolseley's slice, it raised my heart rate and brought a flush to my cheeks that was not only pleasure. My symptoms were a clue to the cake's main drawback. The Battenberg is in fact the only cake on common sale to have been branded a public health risk.

It's all about sugar. In 2018, researchers at Queen Mary University of London tested 381 cakes of twenty-nine types, all bought from the country's leading supermarkets. It's no surprise that most of them were full of sugar, but none was so crammed with the sweet stuff as the Battenberg.

The Oblong of Doom apparently registered up to 62% sugar by weight, compared to an average of 36% in the other cakes tested. A modest 50-gram slice, roughly the size of that reclining elegantly on my plate in Piccadilly, contains more than seven teaspoons of sugar, which is the maximum level that the NHS says an adult human should take on board in an entire day.

The waiter hovered solicitously. Another slice? I declined. My work here, I believed, was done: I had found the True Slice of Battenberg, and honoured the memory of the privileged, accomplished yet ultimately unhappy man who inspired it.

But a second slice at one sitting, my research has made clear, would amount to self-harm. I decided to go home instead, and have a nice lie down.

I couldn't help but feel, however, that my dealings with Battenberg cake were not over. I had paid my respects to the man who inspired it and had eaten a slice of the cake in its finest form. But there was more to the story, because the Victorian Battenberg cake has sprouted as many bizarre descendants as Louis's own family. That sure-fire barometer of the nation's taste, the middle-class maternal online forum Mumsnet, has a lively thread on the mechanics – and indeed mathematics – of scaling up the basic Battenberg, culminating in the suggestion that, for a celebration special Megaberg, one should simply buy a dozen supermarket Battenbergs and stack them up, before covering the pile in a kind of marzipan tarpaulin.

The result, one imagines, would resemble a sugar-based dinosaur dropping, but at least there would be plenty to go round. Because for better or worse, when most British people think of Battenberg cake they imagine the version baked up by a certain Mr Kipling, and I felt it worthwhile, therefore, to ruminate on how this regal cake had become a byword for today's industrialised cake production. The next day, I returned to Mayfair, staying close to the origins of the cake, but on the lookout for its mass-market manifestation.

Just around the corner from the top end of Half Moon Street was a mini-mart. I wandered in and scanned the shelves and there, among the boxed French Fancies and tired croissants, was a single packet of Mr Kipling's Mini Battenbergs.

Fortune – and perhaps the whiskery shade of the late Marquess – was smiling on me. I bought the cakes and walked back down Half Moon Street.

I toyed for a moment with the idea of ringing the bell of No. 42, uninvited. But not only would that have been rude – distinctly un-English – but more significantly I couldn't find No. 42: the doors along this section of the street were black and unadorned with numbers. I settled for a doorstep that was as close as I could get to what I thought was the actual location, sat down, brought out my notebook and unwrapped my packet.

'Cake' is hardly the term for Mr Kipling's shrunken approximation of a Battenberg, but I needed some kind of fuel for my ruminations, and these sticky fingers of chewy, dense sponge, clad in a clammy thin marzipan wrapper and tasting overwhelmingly of sugar, would provide energy, if little else.

CRUMBS OF KNOWLEDGE
INDUSTRIAL CAKES

I may seem dismissive of Mr Kipling's mini-Battenbergs, but I don't wish to be unfair to them, or to their many fans. I had enjoyed a slice of the Wolseley's Battenberg as a treat, but I couldn't afford it every day. Most of us, unless we live with a sweet-toothed expert baker, come across a fine, fresh cake only rarely.

Cake, though, is a huge part of our daily lives, and a hefty slice of the multi-billion-pound British baking industry is devoted to bringing us mass-market cakes, such as a supermarket lemon drizzle, or a plastic-wrapped finger of fruit cake, or one of Mr Kipling's 'Exceedingly good' French Fancies, garishly iced oblongs topped with a blob of buttercream.

Mr Kipling, owned by the giant Premier Foods, is the market-leading brand, but many of the nation's most-consumed cakes are made by vast concerns entirely unheard-of by the public, such as BBF, with factories in the UK and Poland, which works with Marks & Spencer and other supermarkets, and makes, for instance, the M&S Strawberries and Cream Cake. BBF manufacture more than 600 million cakes and desserts annually. Meanwhile, if you buy a birthday cake from a supermarket, it is likely to have been made by Lightbody of Hamilton, Scotland, the UK's leading manufacturer of celebration cakes, who employ more than 1,000 people to make them.

Many of these supermarket cakes are made with ingredients that serious foodies disdain, such as cheap vegetable oils, preservatives and sweeteners, and vast quantities of sugar. And because they are designed – with great care – for mass manufacture, ease of transportation and a certain shelf life, they sometimes lack originality, quirkiness and clarity of flavour. Only one – Colin the Caterpillar, of whom more later – has a story that compelled my attention for this book.

But I don't belittle the pleasure that all of these cakes bring to people's lives, and the remarkable, innovative work that has transformed what was once the treat of the privileged few into the delight of the many.

Mr Kipling himself, by the way, never existed. The brand was invented by advertising whizzes at the J. Walter Thompson agency in 1967, in order to help the bakery giant Rank Hovis McDougall make more money from their flour. 'Kipling' was just one of many names redolent of heritage and empire that was bandied around, and the crucial 'Mr' was added at the suggestion of one of the agency's bright sparks, Llewellyn Thomas, son of the poet Dylan Thomas.

Despite the sugar coursing through my system, I was losing all sensation in my backside. Time for a change of location – and my research had suggested an ideal destination.

I walked north along well-swept pavements, past the gilded frontages of Mayfair and up to Oxford Street. Over that crowded thoroughfare, a left and a right brought me to Edgware Road, which estate agents will try to tell you is the Gateway to the West End. I love it.

I was heading for No. 101, a double-fronted premises under whose generous awnings sat a polyglot gaggle of customers arguing with flatbread over a no-man's-land of hummus, watching football matches on their mobiles while sipping tea, or plugged into hookah pipes in clouds of sweet smoke.

Indoors, it was quieter. Unlike most of the restaurants on this thoroughfare, there were no televisions tuned to Arabic pop or sports channels, just anonymously jangling muzak and painted panels on the walls displaying the cedar trees of Lebanon – which is what the restaurant's name, Al Arez, signifies.

I ordered mint tea, had a look at the uninspiring cakes under glass at the counter and asked for something a bit like a glazed croissant – just as a decoy, you understand.

When all had been delivered by a smiling, rapid, over-worked waiter, I surreptitiously produced a mini-Battenberg from the packet in my pocket and popped it on to the plate next to the pastry, then brought out my notebook once more.

A mouthful of mini-Battenberg – Mr Kipling's version now positively cloying – provided a sugar-rush of mental energy. Which is just as well, because I had discovered that the story of the cake's origins is almost as complex as the story of Louis's ancestry – and there are a final few twists to unfurl.

Most sources that I had seen cite the Battenberg marriage story without quibble, though often spelling the name 'Battenburg'. And many cite as the earliest written evidence of the cake its appearance in A. G. Bromley's *Book of Cakes* of 1903. Another popular theory, repeated, for example, on *The Great British Bake Off* (Series 2, Episode 1), is that the four squares of the cake represent four Battenberg (or 'burg') princes: Louis himself and his brothers Alexander, Franz-Joseph and Henry.

That's probably not true. But it is certainly the case that the chequerboard pattern is responsible for a weird offshoot of the Battenberg legend, as the name is now an accepted shorthand term for the dayglo-squares paint job seen on police and other rapid response vehicles.

The most convincing account of the Battenberg cake origin story pooh-poohs the myth of the four brothers and establishes an earlier source for the first recipe.

The food historian Ivan Day has found two earlier recipes for the cake, both recorded in published print by a man named Frederick Vine.

Vine was a late-nineteenth-century Paul Hollywood, the author of numerous books, the editor of the trade magazine *The British Baker*, and the proprietor of a substantial business preparing, according to his publicity material, 'fancy bread' and biscuits, Viennoiserie, pastries, jellies and ices, and of course cakes: 'Genoa, Pound, Madeira... and other cakes of very superior quality.'

Mr Vine was to be found supervising his staff and charming his customers, ensuring that all could be prepared at the shortest notice and that all orders were 'punctually attended to' in his splendid premises at 101 Edgware Road, on the very spot where Al Arez now stands, and where I tucked into my tiny sugary, inferior versions of the very cake that Frederick Vine first identified in print.

In a way. The first cake that Vine confidently describes as 'Battenburg Cake', No. 84 in his book *Cakes and How to Make Them*, published around 1890, is in fact a straightforward fruit cake baked in a loaf tin. Nice enough in its own way, rammed with juicy sultanas and sharpened with mixed peel, but not remotely like anything that we know as a Battenberg cake. A decoy.

Vine's next effort is much closer to what we know now. This ascribes the Battenburg name to a cake with nine, rather than four, panels. It is published – with a rudimentary but unmistakable illustration – in *Saleable Shop Goods*, a sort of how-to book for professional bakers that appeared in 1898.

What Vine does not say is that the cake was invented, or renamed, in honour of the royal wedding of Louis and Princess Victoria – which took place just fourteen years before his book came out. Nor have I been able to find any printed source contemporary with the wedding that confirms the reason for the cake's name. Vine's nine-panel number certainly seems to finish off the idea that the four panels might represent the four Battenberg brothers – unless satirical bakers were referring to illegitimate siblings...

No doubt more evidence will turn up one day. Meanwhile the circumstantial case for the commemorative naming is overwhelming, as is the lack of any alternative argument. But there are reasons to believe that opportunist Victorian bakers simply modified existing cakes to come up with a tribute to the newly-weds.

Ivan Day, the food sleuth who discovered the first mention of the nine-panel 'Battenburg', did not stop there. Delving deeper into the archives, he came across a recipe for what was called 'Neapolitan Roll', in *Cakes and Buns* by one Robert Wells, which was published in Manchester in (most likely) 1897.

Unlike the nine-panel Battenburg, the Neapolitan Roll is a dead ringer for the Battenberg cake that we know now: four panels of sponge, two plain and two pink, spread with jam and encased in marzipan – the only point of difference being a thin disguise of pink desiccated coconut dusted all over the marzipan shell.

History records, then, that the first Battenburg cake had the wrong spelling and the wrong number of sponge panels; while the first Battenberg cake that we might instantly recognise was disguised by a pink overcoat and another name altogether.

It's a convoluted tale, befitting a cake named after a man of many names, ranks and titles.

But at least Louis/Ludwig had actually existed, which is more than can be said for Mr Kipling. From a real royal to a fictional baker, and from the corridors of power to the confectionery aisle of Tesco: Battenberg had come a long way, and I felt that I had too. Time for another lie down.

BATTENBERG CAKE

As I have suggested, this cake is one that seems to invite weird (and not always wonderful) improvisation. This is an excellent and respectable version from Rose Prince, a knowledgeable and witty cook and food writer whose work I have admired for many years, who blogs at roseprince.co.uk and is on Instagram at roseprincecooks. Rose recommends artificial food colouring in this case, as she has found that vegetable-based colouring can fade disappointingly in the cooking.

If you wish to get a little closer to the spirit of the Wolseley, substitute apricot jam for strawberry.

You will need two 1kg loaf tins, buttered, bases lined with parchment, then buttered again and dusted lightly with flour

280g softened butter

280g caster sugar

5 eggs

280g self-raising flour

1 tbsp milk

1–2 tsp artificial pink food colouring

CAKE

To assemble

approximately 150g strawberry jam, blended or sieved

225g ready-to-use marzipan

1. Preheat the oven to 180°C/350°F/Gas Mark 4.
2. Cream the butter and sugar in a large bowl, using an electric beater or a wooden spoon, until pale-coloured. Add 1 egg at a time, beating well before adding each one. Fold in the flour with the milk, making sure it is well incorporated.
3. Divide the mixture between two bowls. Add the food colouring to one, blending it in thoroughly or your cake will have a marbled appearance. Turn the pink batter into one cake tin, and the yellow into the other. Bake for 40 minutes, or until the cakes are springy to the touch and a skewer inserted comes out clean.
4. Turn out the cakes on to a rack and allow to cool completely. Using a sharp, thin-bladed serrated knife, cut each cake into identical-sized rectangles, about 5 x 5 x 20cm. Spread with jam to stick the pieces together in two tiers of two.
5. Finally, spread jam on all four sides of the cake. Roll out the marzipan to no more than ½cm thickness. Trim to size and wrap the cake, which is then ready to slice.

CHAPTER 6
CHRISTMAS CAKE AND TWELFTH CAKE

One day in early December 1965 – or perhaps 1966, none of the survivors concerned in this story can confirm the year, though they are quite certain about the circumstances – a lady of some seventy years of age waited at a bus stop on Hadley Green on the outskirts of Barnet, just north of London.

She was sensibly dressed and armed against the cold, with warm boots, a woolly hat and mittens. She carried a large, apparently empty shopping bag, and from time to time she took from it a timetable for the Green Line bus service, which she squinted at through her steamed-up glasses.

Red double-decker buses pulled up at the stop, but these were of no interest to her. The lady – who was called Elsie Martin, and was my maternal grandmother – was concerned only with the much less frequent Green Line bus, which connected the distant suburbs of south London with their northern counterparts via King's Cross and, among other places, Hadley Green.

Each time one of these pulled up at the stop, Mrs Martin waited for one or two passengers to step off, then climbed aboard and fixed the driver with a gimlet eye.

'Do you have a package for the Bakers?' she would demand.

'A package, madam?' each driver would respond. 'I'm afraid not.'

Several of the drivers – by my grandmother's telling – were more forthright in their response, pointing out to her that they carried passengers, not packages. 'Take a look at my hat, dearie,' one driver had the temerity to suggest. 'It says Green Line, doesn't it? Not Royal Mail...'

Three or four times the lady returned to the pavement, cold externally but inwardly heated by rising indignation. My grandmother had been born in the East End of London in the reign of Queen Victoria, when Louis Battenberg was in his prime. She had survived two World Wars and did not suffer fools – or impertinent bus drivers – gladly.

Eventually, at perhaps the fifth or sixth attempt, Mrs Martin got the response she wanted. 'Yes!' The Green Line driver responded. 'I do have a package for the Bakers. Just a minute...' And he rummaged around, or perhaps even under, his seat, producing a hefty oblong wrapped in brown paper and tied with string, and addressed in large capital letters thus:

Mr Richard Baker and Family. By Hand.

'Thank you,' said my grandmother, stowing the parcel with care in her shopping bag and favouring the driver with her kindest smile. 'Most obliging of you, I'm sure.'

And she descended to the pavement and set across the Green, and the driver shut his doors, and called out, 'Hold very tight please,' and set out for St Albans, or perhaps Harpenden. He may well have been shaking his head and thinking that he could tell his pals back at the depot that today he had delivered not only his passengers to his destinations, but a Christmas cake to a television newsreader.

One of the main reasons this story is remembered and passed down the generations is the instant picture it summons of my strong-willed grandmother fuming on the chilly pavement as bus after bus halted and passed on without cake. She may also have muttered about her daughter, housebound nearby caring for her infant son and new baby, and her son-in-law, no doubt gallivanting around at the BBC and thus unable to collect the cake addressed to him.

I – the infant son – was barely old enough to form permanent memories at the time, but the incident has stuck, yet another instance of cake's ability to summon memories. Usually, as Diane Purkiss, Oxford professor of English and food historian, has noted, pleasant memories. 'Cake is often seen as offering a window to a more stable past,' she points out – though in the context of religious practices, rather than Green Line buses.

The cake delivered by the bus driver had been made by the housekeeper of a lady called Mary Harper, a south London spinster of substantial means who had taken a shine to my father through the medium of television and sent him occasional letters and modest gifts by post.

Her housekeeper was a fine cook, renowned for her Christmas cakes, and Miss Harper resolved to send one of these to her favourite newscaster. For some reason she was unwilling to entrust the Royal Mail with the finished item, and was stuck for a solution until the housekeeper mentioned her nephew, a Green Line bus driver often employed on the Croydon to Hertfordshire route, which passed providentially close to our house in Hadley Highstone.

Goodness only knows how all of this detail became clear or how the plan was hatched – we should bear in mind, perhaps, that apart from precious news bulletins there was little to watch on television at this time – but the cake was baked, the bus driver was recruited, and all went according to plan.

If this were a novel I should be able to conclude this passage with the cutting of the cake and the presentation of a slice to my four-year-old self, a flood of memories released at the recollection of that confection.

Unfortunately I have neither the fictional gifts of Monsieur Proust, nor any specific recollection of Mary Harper's housekeeper's cake. All that I recall of the Christmas cakes of my extreme youth – Miss Harper's included – is white icing like a choppy frozen sea, in which were embedded blobby, vaguely festive figures, formed from plaster or some early plastic and primitively painted: a trio of children on a sledge, a penguin with a broken beak and a Santa figure on a kind of plinth, his featureless head thrown back in silent jollity.

I remember the decorations and the icing rather than the cake because my infant brother and myself were not interested in the cake, still less the horrid marzipan that separated the cake from the sugary snowdrifts above: it was the icing we were after, fascinated equally by the mission of chipping Santa and his pals free from their concrete-hard surroundings, and eating as much of the surroundings as we could before we were rumbled.

The elements of a Christmas cake have changed not at all in the half century and more since Mary Harper's housekeeper got to work on our behalf.

In this century, people are infinitely more likely to buy such a cake than to make it, or to receive one from a friend (or besotted fan). Every supermarket has an aisle stacked with their interpretation of the festive bake.

But despite the advances in baking and decoration technology, Christmas cake is little changed from the time of my grandmother, or her grandmother – a contemporary of Charles Dickens.

Indeed, while birthday cake has transmogrified into an anthropomorphic caterpillar and wedding cake has morphed into a tower of buttercreamed cylinders, Christmas cake, like Dundee cake, is a living link to the great cakes of the past.

The Yuletide version was known to generations of Britons as Twelfth Cake, intended to be the centrepiece of the celebrations of Twelfth Night, the 5th of January, the last night of Christmas and the culmination of a dozen days of festivities and feasting. Early versions of these cakes, such as those that might have been prepared for a Tudor Christmas, were decorated with marzipan (or 'marchpane') toppings, often in sculptural form. The layer of snowy sugar was a much later innovation as imports rose, costs fell and refining technology improved.

CRUMBS OF KNOWLEDGE
PUDDING OR CAKE?

For clarity, I should point out the difference between Christmas pudding, the item often brought flaming to the table and consumed with lashings of cream and brandy butter, and Christmas cake. The former is a pudding, traditionally made with suet and steamed rather than baked. It is well suited to being doused with cheap brandy and set alight but, being a pudding, has no place in this book. The latter is a cake, baked and then decorated with marzipan and icing, which under no circumstances should be set alight but which is fully entitled to be included here.

By the mid-Victorian era the strict observance of the Twelve Days of Christmas had fallen away, not least because everyone was working too hard to be able to spare the time for it. But those aspirational toilers were fascinated by Twelfth Cakes, and London bakers competed to assemble the most extravagant examples for their shop windows.

Dickens's *A Christmas Carol*, first published in 1843, is the most important single work in establishing the nature of the English Christmas in the public mind. The author didn't invent Christmas, but such was the influence of his work – among his contemporaries and since – that his stamp of approval preserved some ancient customs in the public mind, discarded others, boosted the popularity of the turkey over the goose, and suffused everything with a feel-good golden glow.

Twelfth Cake is there, mentioned admiringly not only in the text but also in the first illustrations, where the Spirit of Christmas Present, a jolly, bare-chested figure in a green gown like an off-duty rugby player, rests a bare foot upon a vast Twelfth Cake a yard wide and a foot tall.

Such cakes were a source of pride for those who were able to buy and serve them, or who had servants to make them; and they were a source of wonder to entire communities, who flocked around bakers' shop windows to gaze in awe at the giant confections in the run-up to the festivities.

So central were the cakes to the jollity that traditions grew up around the crowds who came to gawp at them. The author William Hone, in his *Every Day Book*, records not only the 'countless cakes of all prices and dimensions, that stand in rows and piles on the counters and sideboards, and in the windows' of the bakers' shops, but also the gangs of boys playing Twelfth Night tricks on the cake-watchers, nailing their coat-tails to the shop window frames and pinning together pairs of strangers. 'At every nailing and pinning shouts of laughter arise from the perpetrators and the spectators,' Hone records, until the constables have to be called.

As new cake-related traditions evolved, old ones faded away. The great Christmas cake of yore was not simply a tasty treat to be consumed, but a focus for the evening's entertainment. Twelfth Night was an excuse for wild celebration, when rich and poor mingled and social rank was briefly upended.

The riotous tone of the evening was set not by the Lord and Lady of the hosting household, but by the King and Queen of Misrule, selected by means of the cake, which always concealed, baked into its depths, a dried pea and a dried bean. If a male guest found the bean he would become the King for the evening; while a woman who found the pea would become Queen. If a woman found the bean, she got to choose the King. If a man found the pea, he got to choose the Queen. Everyone in the household, as well as all guests, were included in the ceremony of the cake, and if the household servants won the right to be Kings or Queens even their masters had to obey.

Historians have suggested that this Twelfth Night inversion of social roles was a medieval hangover from Dark Ages traditions that were themselves shadowy recollections of the rituals of the Roman colonisers. The Roman Saturnalia, celebrated in late December, included the practice of hiding a dried bean in a cake to select the ruler of the household for the duration of the festivities.

As centuries passed, and as the quality of cake ingredients and cooking technology improved, people became less keen to spoil their beautiful cakes by scrabbling around in them for prizes; by the time of Samuel Pepys in the seventeenth century, the cake was to be admired, and eaten, while the social roles were ascribed by drawing lots. On 6 January 1669, Pepys reports that he served his guests 'a noble cake', and 'to prevent spoiling the cake' wrote the character titles on pieces of paper and drew them from a hat.

In Dickens's time there were model figures representing the King and Queen, and sets of printed cards with caricatures of the assorted cast of party characters that could be shuffled and handed out without the need to disturb the elaborate Twelfth Cake.

By the time of my first Christmases, the festival had shrunk from Twelve Days to a couple. The term 'Twelfth Cake' had encompassed many variations on the theme of the decorated fruit cake, but what had unified them all was the date on which they were intended to be consumed. As Twelfth Night lost importance, Twelfth Cake became Christmas cake, and the ancient notion that food could contain or bestow luck or good fortune migrated from the cake to the Christmas pudding, which at our Christmas lunches always contained a sixpence, wrapped by my cautious mother in tinfoil and inserted before the pudding was steamed. Whoever discovered the coin in their slice (and it wasn't hard to find) earned not the right to command the household, alas, but good luck for the year ahead – a blessing that had always been forgotten in the rush to consume the pudding and decamp to the dining room in time for the Queen's televised Christmas message.

Today's Christmas cake is itself a kind of ghost of Christmas past, a shrunken imitation of the behemoths of olden times, and a treat that has lost not only its original name, but also its date of consumption and its role in the household.

Surely I can't be alone in standing in the supermarket in the run-up to Christmas and thinking, 'Turkey, check; pudding, check; mince pies, check; Christmas cake... well, OK. But why?'

This question becomes more insistent every year in late October and early November, when in the newspaper office where I work we find ourselves surrounded by every retailable manifestation of Christmas food to be 'tried and tested'. My colleague Tomé Morrissy-Swan, the *Telegraph*'s Assistant Food Editor, a mild-mannered, omnivorous yet slender young man, is in charge of accumulating mountains of festive grub, assessing them, and then distributing them among colleagues and local charities to ensure that none goes to waste.

So on Tuesday, for instance, we might find him gamely slogging through a dozen portions of vegetarian stuffing; the next day ranks of mince pies will be lined up for his attention, while on Thursday he will tuck into vegan pigs in blankets. He deserves a medal, but whoever pins it on had better take care not to cause an almighty explosion.

The assembled Christmas cakes piled up for his attention all around his desk looked like the ramparts of a children's fort: sturdy square cartons in festive scarlet and green with plastic windows to reveal the shiny white confections within.

Tomé, who is a good height, was all but invisible behind the cartons. Every so often his hands would appear to move one from atop the pile on to his desk for tasting, or swap a couple around. Colleagues passed by with amused glances, many of them observing, 'Someone's got to do it!' as if it were an original line. 'Ho ho ho,' Tomé replied, entirely without humour.

While he chewed and savoured and made notes about icing thickness behind his wall of festive packaging, I crept up and examined the boxes. Soon I'd volunteer to help with the tasting – we all had to do our bit – but first I wanted to have a look at the language of Christmas cake marketing.

The first thing I noticed was that the term 'Christmas' was rarely used: the C-word appearing on only four of the fourteen cakes that were being tasted. Instead shops either went for adjectives redolent of deep midwinter – 'Shimmering'; 'Frosty'; or evocative of the ingredients: 'Luxury'; 'Rich' and, less ambitiously, 'Fully Iced'.

One key ingredient was more prominent than any other: cakes were 'Laced with brandy' or 'Brandy-soaked' or, in the case of Aldi's offering, both 'brandy soaked' and 'brandy infused', with an additional picture of a brandy bottle for those customers who might have been too pickled to read.

As for the cakes themselves... you may have read the results, if not in the *Telegraph*, then in the *Guardian*, *The Times*, *Good Housekeeping*, the *Liverpool Echo* or *Catering Week*. Or any of the countless media outlets that consider the annual Christmas Cake Taste Test to be a sure-fire audience-pleaser year after year, especially if – as is often the case – tasters prefer a budget offering to one from a 'posh' retailer.

What I really wanted to do was to pick Tomé's sugar-addled brain in my own pursuit of the True Slice. I made a token effort to help him out with the tasting, sampling a couple of cakes and murmuring 'fruity' and 'hefty' and then, as he sat back surrounded by debris of dried fruit and crumbs of icing, I ventured a question.

In the light of his day's tasting, what was his idea of the ideal Christmas cake?

'Omigod.'

I see. Could you... expand on that at all?

'I need to take a break. Excuse me.'

The next day, when his natural colour had returned, I asked Tomé what it had been like to sample more than a dozen Christmas cakes at one sitting.

'It was quite challenging,' he said. This from a veteran of comparative brownie marathons and breakfast-toastie taste-offs.

'The thing about Christmas cake is that they are all setting out to seem rich.' He winced at the recollection and I understood at once what he was getting at. I have yet to see a Christmas cake or its multi-faith winter-festive equivalent marketed as a Lite option.

It perhaps had not helped that Tomé was a latecomer to the Christmas cake, having been brought up in a wonderfully multicultural family with elements of Brazilian, British, Polish and Jewish culinary culture; but a household in which almond-based confectionery didn't feature.

'I don't know why, but it was a marzipan-free zone,' he said. 'At Christmas we always went for pudding rather than cake, so I never tasted marzipan when I was a child, and when I first had some as an adult, I hated it.'

And... now? 'I was coming round to it, but I think I'll give it a miss for the next month or so.'

I was still on a mission, though. With the benefit of twenty-four hours of consideration – and indeed digestion – what qualities had an expert taster been looking for in the Christmas cakes, and what had he found?

'You want balance in a sophisticated cake. Fruit, a nut or two for texture, a hint of spice but not too much, a certain level of booziness. I think citrus is important in any kind of Christmas dessert, and not just from candied peel. It mustn't be dry; I like the texture to be closer to pudding than cake if possible.' Frankly, he'd rather eat Christmas pudding than Christmas cake. 'True. But that wasn't this week's job.' What a trouper.

His general impression was that supermarket cakes were light on marzipan and heavy on icing, which he reckoned may well have a lot to do with the relative cost of ground almonds and icing sugar; that moistness was elusive and that booziness, even when promised, had usually evaporated long ago.

Tomé's favourite was Asda's offering, which he liked because of its orange – the fruit, not the colour – marzipan, 'which brings me back to that thing of Christmas citrus. A bit of zest, a bit of sharpness, a bit of warmth.'

A strong candidate for the True Slice, then? Tomé pointed out that it was a fine exponent of the modern Christmas cake: 'brandy-soaked and fully iced', and also, according to the box, generously filled with vine fruits and glacé cherries, and enriched with warming spices.

Job done, you might have thought: napkin on.

But I had seen this cake while Tomé had been tasting, and I had him dig the remaining half of it out of a Tupperware container. I nibbled on a corner, and it was as he had said, a fine cake. But that wasn't the issue. I pulled out a ruler from the depths of my desk. Asda's Extra Special Fully Iced Fruit Cake was 45mm or, in terms that Dickens would understand, barely more than an inch and a half tall. I was looking for a Twelfth Cake. This was more like one-sixteenth.

What I had in mind was more along the lines of Queen Victoria's Twelfth Cake, captured by an artist's impression in the *Illustrated London News* in 1849. This iced behemoth, bulging at the equator as if ready to burst, was 30 inches across and almost double that in height, once you had taken into account the sugarwork picnic scene – complete with pine trees – on its ample top surface.

Not easily portable, though. But from his pile Tomé turned up a cake which, though much more modest in proportions, retained the spirit of the Victorian Twelfth. The Authentic Bread Company's Organic Iced Christmas Cake had the right proportions – depth as well as width – and was crowned not only with a good slap of icing but also with a hefty intervening layer of marzipan.

The True Slice. But where to eat in an authentic manner?

'That's difficult. I mean...' Tomé looked around a little nervously, even though there were no children in the newsroom '... a lot of Christmas is invented, isn't it?'

Good point. I could go to the North Pole, but I wouldn't find Santa there, or any Christmas cake. I could probably find Santa – or at least a version of him – and cake, at Harrods. But they wouldn't be true, in any sense apart from truly expensive. I could eat it at home, but that would just be a cop-out.

'I know!' Tomé cried. He had been tapping away at his PC. 'Winter Wonderland. Opens on Friday. Just down the road.'

Some kind of awful festive serendipity had been at work. I loathe and detest Winter Wonderland, a sprawling cross between a funfair and a German Christmas market, which squats on a vast chunk of Hyde Park for three winter months. I scoff and scowl as I plod past it on my walk home on evenings in late November and throughout December. How many times have I held forth on my disdain for it? How often have I declared that I would rather chop off a leg and feed it to Santa's reindeer than set foot in that fairy-lit hellscape?

Yet I couldn't deny that Tomé – or perhaps the spirit of modern Christmas speaking through his cake-addled form – had pronounced a just sentence. At this stage in the Yuletide quest, I felt I needed a single location that summed up the contemporary experience of Christmas, in all its commercial gaudiness. To Winter Wonderland I must go.

'Perhaps they'll have a cake stall,' Tomé said. But he didn't sound very optimistic. 'I'll bundle you up a couple of slices of Authentic Organic anyway.'

So it was that, having recruited my elder daughter Lucy for company, I approached the Red Gate to Winter Wonderland one evening in mid-November. I was nervous. Not just at the prospect of what lay ahead inside the gates, but at the prospect of being denied entry on account of the sizeable lump of Christmas cake concealed about my person.

Bags were being inspected by unsmiling security personnel. Certain persons were being given polite but thorough pat-downs. I was aware that customers were explicitly forbidden from bringing a great many specific items into the wondrous compound, mostly for understandable reasons

('Knives... air-horns... distress flares... Drug Paraphernalia including Psychoactive Substances... motorbikes, quad bikes and buggies... corrosive substances including acids... kites and musical instruments...'), and while Christmas cake was not specifically mentioned on the banned list, I didn't want an awkward conversation about the psychoactive potential of marzipan.

It was OK. I might have felt suspicious, but I obviously didn't look it, and we passed the gate-guards without interrogation or intrusive searches.

My main purpose was to scout the place thoroughly for Christmas cake, since I reckoned that any actually sold on the premises would be authentic, or at least authentically phony, and thus a candidate for the True Slice. My inside pocket contents were the evening's back-up plan.

Lucy's main purpose was to obtain one of the gigantic spherical furry animals, a yard or so in diameter, that were being lugged around the grounds by parents, having been won by their children at fairground stalls.

My first-born child is now in her mid-twenties and has several degrees and a responsible public service job, but show her a giant beachball wrapped in fake fur with a goofy face on it and she regresses instantly.

Never mind. We made a deal. If she assisted me in my cake search, I would sponsor her attempts to throw things at other things until she won a furry grinning blimp.

First, though, we went to the Ice Palace. There wasn't going to be any cake in there, but I wanted value for my £7.50 entrance fee and I didn't want to get it by being hurled around on a festive horror ride, twirled on a big wheel or tormented in a Hall of Mirrors.

The Ice Palace was unchallenging in any physical sense apart from the fact that, being effectively a giant freezer cabinet in a marquee, it was very, very cold. We were dressed for a mild evening, so that by the time we had nodded approvingly at the tableaux of forest animals, the knights in armour and the sleeping princesses, all carved most impressively from crystal clear ice, our teeth were chattering and the charm was wearing off as our core temperatures plunged.

We took a short cut through a castle-style gateway made entirely of ice (quite impressive actually), climbed stairs (not made of ice) to what I thought was the exit, and instead found ourselves at the top of an ice slide, which was undignified and monstrously cold on the nether regions.

Then we were back out into the mild November evening, searching countless tacky stalls in Angel's Christmas Market for signs of cake.

Without success. One little shack – the only one claiming to be any kind of cake specialist – had a dreadful sort of bundt thing and a nondescript panettone, but that was it. Otherwise there were acres of sweet stalls hawking yards of lurid chewy laces, cotton candy that looked like loft insulation and smiley-face lollipops the size of clockfaces.

'Look!' exclaimed Lucy. 'The skating rink is sponsored by Lidl! Classy.'

I sponsored Lucy £10, which got her ten squidgy balls to bounce into a bucket in order to win a cuddly, crazy-faced blimp. She succeeded with her first ball, much to the annoyance of the teenagers standing next to her... who changed their tune when she donated them her leftover balls.

With Lucy toting a fuzzy animal the size of a dishwasher, we headed for the food village in search of sustenance. The daughter decided on a huge, suspicious-looking sausage prepared by an unsmiling geezer with comic-book Germanic moustaches. While she sprayed this with dayglo sauce and devoured it, I surreptitiously unwrapped a chunk of my smuggled traditional Christmas cake.

Standing next to the sausage stall ('Mr Bratwurst') with an excellent view of a dazzling funhouse called Archibald, Master of Time, Vol. 2, I nibbled at my cake. It was quite nice, moist crumb, though not over-generous with fruit or marzipan layer.

But the point was that I could not have felt less Christmassy if I had been in central Tehran in June.

The whole set-up was ersatz, gimcrack, fake and generally rubbish, and put me solidly in character as Ebenezer Scrooge before he had those chats with the ghosts.

'I wish I hadn't had that sausage,' Lucy said. 'Can we go home?'

I needed a Plan B, and thinking of Scrooge – indeed, thinking like Scrooge – had given me an idea. Nothing I could put into action that evening, but I had plenty of Christmas cake left over, and plenty of time left before Christmas.

We set off for the bus stop, Lucy lugging her vast prize and essaying cautious, sausagey burps.

The problem with my first attempt at a True Slice of Christmas Cake in an Authentic Location had been all about the inauthenticity of the location. Yes, for some Winter Wonderland sums up the contemporary Christmas experience but, to me, it didn't feel remotely Christmassy. Right cake, right time, or not far off. Wrong place.

So my solution was to abandon the modern Yuletide experience – which is horrible – and seek an authentic slice of Dickensian Christmas life.

I'm not going to get too tangled up in layers of meaning, generational appropriation and historiographical debate here. Leaving aside the religious aspect – clearly central but of limited relevance in this context – Christmas as we experience it is a stocking full of traditions from different times and different cultures, from the pagan Holly King of my Anglo-Saxon adventures, through the gigantic Twelfth Cake of the Middle Ages to the multicultural greedfest in Hyde Park.

Anyone who takes an interest in Christmas has their own angle on it and their own favourite aspect of the celebrations: I may not like Winter Wonderland but I understand why tens of thousands of people love it; my wife is unlikely to attend Midnight Mass but loves nothing more than a prettily decorated festive table and a vast light-festooned tree.

I get a shiver down my spine at the first note of the treble solo that opens the carol service from King's College Chapel in Cambridge, the official start of the festivities as far as I am concerned, and I am a sucker for Christmas Past: a fire in the grate, snow mantling the eaves, a bowl of steaming punch for my jolly neighbours... the whole Dickensian nine yards, in fact.

So my True Slice of Christmas cake would be eaten in that sort of context, and since I had an authentic-ish cake, the only snag was that none of those circumstances are manifest in my own house over the festive season: we don't have a fire, or eaves, it never snows at Christmas and while my neighbours are jolly they don't drink punch (champagne, for preference; prosecco at a push).

Fortunately, the Dickens Museum is not far away, and they have the most authentic Dickensian setting one can possibly imagine: his house. And, as you might expect, they know how to do Christmas.

I walked down to the Dickens House in Doughty Street from Chancery Lane tube station shortly after opening time one cold Wednesday morning not long after the Winter Wonderland debacle. A small square of Tomé's Authentic Organic, wrapped in non-PVC clingfilm, nestled in my coat pocket.

It is not an especially grand or imposing dwelling: a Georgian terraced house, one among many such on this handsome street. It is the only one of the author's London houses that survives, but Dickens didn't live here long, just two and half years between March 1837 and December 1839.

It was a busy time, though. In the modest study overlooking the little garden in Doughty Street, Dickens finished *The Pickwick Papers*, wrote most of *Oliver Twist*, all of *Nicholas Nickleby*, and started *Barnaby Rudge*, all the while editing a magazine, writing articles, giving speeches, campaigning, socialising and bringing up a family.

Celebrating Christmas was a big part of family life. In an essay on the Dickens Museum website, Pen Vogler writes that 'Dickens was indubitably king of the Twelfth Night revels, recalled his daughter Mamie; he called on every one to join in the songs, recitations and theatricals; and "under his attentions the shyest child would brighten and become merry".

Cake was unquestionably part of the fun: we know that Dickens's friend, the philanthropist Angela Burdett-Coutts, used to send the Dickens family a vast Twelfth Cake every year: the author once joked that it weighed ninety pounds.

And it is clear from his work that the author was fascinated by the festival. Everyone knows about Scrooge and the ghosts, but their tale was just one of many Christmas stories that Dickens wrote, employing the season and its traditions as a kind of magnifying glass for his characters and their attitudes.

Miserliness and generosity, for example, fall into much clearer relief in the context of Christmas, when the needs of the humble and hungry may be contrasted so starkly with the opulence and splendour of the feasts of the better off.

His own house would have been splendidly decorated, with recently cut evergreen leaves set off by scarlet ribbons, to judge from the arrangements that I saw in the house when I visited. In Dickens's day there would have been a roaring fire in every grate, too, but alas, Health and Safety decreed that only a glowing imitation sat under the mantelpiece in the first-floor drawing room when I entered.

But let me dwell on what was there: magnificently, almost magically. Without any pre-arrangement or request for favours, the friendly volunteer who ushered me – alone, blissfully – into the drawing room indicated a low armchair by the fire.

'Have a seat, if you like,' she said. 'Pick up the book. You're welcome to read a little.'

I did as she suggested, hardly daring to reach for the little red clothbound hardback, so strongly did I wish for it to be one title in particular.

'Ohhhh...' How wonderful. It was *A Christmas Carol*.

The volunteer had left the room. I felt in my coat pocket and discreetly freed a morsel of cake. In my left hand I held the little old book, open to the first page of the story. With my right I popped the morsel of cake into my mouth. Crumbs and squashy fruit, a hint of spice, flavours and aromas of Christmas. The cold, grey street outside was quiet; in the cosy room the lights seemed to flicker and dim, and I read: 'Marley was dead...'

It was a powerful moment, deeply pleasurable, resonant and moving, and a vindication of the quest. I felt that I had involved all of my senses, sitting there by the fireplace in Doughty Street, in a house that clearly fires the powers of imagination in all who cross the threshold. With a mouthful of cake, I had surely stirred a ghost of Christmas Past.

I shut my eyes and my mind skittered back to the Christmas cakes of my childhood, like the one that my grandmother had waited for at the bus stop. Cake was working its time machine magic again, conjuring fragmentary memories of small, booted feet in thick snow, of gifts bulging in thick woollen socks beside a fireplace, flanking a chimney down which, I truly believed, Santa would descend.

Christmas Present – at least in the form of Winter Wonderland – holds no magic for me. My children are grown up, and it never seems to snow. The best Christmases are those in the past. And cake can take me there.

CHRISTMAS CAKE WITH QUINCE

This recipe, a little unusual and very delicious, is by my wise and kindly friend and long-standing Telegraph *colleague Xanthe Clay, with whom I have shared many culinary journeys and adventures. The quince and mincemeat – as in mince pie – elements make, Xanthe says, 'for an ultra-moist cake with lots of interesting flavours and textures'. She also says that it is fairly easy, so don't be panicked by the length of the recipe.*

**MAKES ONE 20cm CAKE –
ABOUT 22cm ONCE ICED**

125g butter

125g dark muscovado sugar

5 tbsp sloe gin, plus 4 tbsp to spoon over at the end

grated zest and juice of 1 orange

grated zest of 1 lemon and juice of ½

50g apricots, snipped into 2 or 3

50g dried sour cherries

100g currants

100g golden raisins

100g sultanas

100g figs, snipped into 3 (throw away the stalks)

1 quince, about 250g, poached with 75g caster sugar
(see recipe below)

100g crystallised ginger

50g blanched hazelnuts

50g candied peel, chopped (optional)

3 large eggs

100g ground almonds

1 tsp ground nutmeg

1 tsp grated cinnamon

8 cardamom pods, bashed in a pestle and mortar
with a fat pinch of salt

150g self-raising flour

around 200g quince cheese (Waitrose or Fine Cheese Co.
versions are good)

1. Double line a 20cm round cake tin with baking
parchment.
2. Put the butter, muscovado sugar, 5 tablespoons of
sloe gin, and the citrus zest and juice into a pan and
heat gently until the butter has melted. Add the dried
fruit and simmer for 10 minutes. Turn off the heat
and leave to cool.
3. Preheat the oven to 150°C/300°F/Gas Mark 2.
4. Add the quince, ginger, hazelnuts, candied peel (if
using), eggs, ground almonds, nutmeg and cinnamon
to the fruit mixture. Fish out any cardamom husks
from the cardamom salt and add the rest to the bowl.
Stir to mix, then sift over the flour and fold in.

5. Spoon half the mixture carefully into the tin. Slice the quince cheese and lay it over the top – leaving a rim of 1cm around the edge. Spoon the rest of the cake mixture over the top, and level off.

6. Bake the cake for 45 minutes, then turn the heat down to 140°C/275°F/Gas Mark 1 and bake for another 1–1½ hours, or until a skewer plunged into the middle comes out without raw mixture on it.

7. Take the cake out of the oven and skewer it all over the top. Pour on the last 4 tablespoons of sloe gin. Leave to cool in the tin, then wrap well in a layer of greaseproof paper and a layer of foil. Store in an airtight container for up to a month. You can 'feed' the cake with 4 more tablespoons of sloe gin every couple of weeks if you like.

— HAZELNUT MARZIPAN —

300g roast ground hazelnuts

30g liquid glucose

100g icing sugar

100g caster sugar

50g beaten egg

5 tbsp quince jelly or apricot jam, heated gently and rubbed through a sieve (to stick on the marzipan)

1. Blend the hazelnuts, glucose, icing sugar, caster sugar and beaten egg in a food processor to form a thick dough. Add a little more beaten egg if necessary to bring it all together. Tip it on to the work surface and knead briefly. Wrap well and chill until ready to use. Bring to room temperature before rolling.
2. Brush the cake with the jelly or jam.
3. Roll the marzipan out to about 8mm thick. Cut a circle just over 20cm across and lay it over the top of the cake, easing down the edges. Cut a strip to fit the side – you can do this in several pieces – and press around the sides. Use your fingers to smooth together the seams. Leave to dry for 3–5 days.

— ROYAL ICING —

3 large egg whites
600g icing sugar
10g liquid glucose
1 tsp lemon juice

1. Beat the egg whites until frothy, then, with the beaters still running, add the icing sugar a spoonful at a time. When it is all incorporated, add the glucose and lemon juice and beat until you have a thick snowy mass.
2. Spread over the cake, smoothing with a palette knife. Leave to set for at least 24 hours.

— POACHED QUINCE —

1 quince, about 250g, washed, cored and cut into approx.
2½cm cubes (no need to peel it)

75g sugar

grated zest of ½ lemon

1 vanilla pod

1. Put all the ingredients into a small pan with about
   300ml water; add a bit more if it doesn't quite cover
   the fruit. (You can tie the trimmings and core of the
   quince in a muslin bag and put them into the pan too,
   if you like: it will improve the texture and flavour if
   you do.)
2. Bring slowly to simmering point, allowing the sugar
   to dissolve.
3. Cover and simmer very gently for at least an hour
   (up to 2 hours), until the quince is tawny, then
   remove the lid and continue simmering until the
   liquid has mostly evaporated – a few drops on a cold
   saucer will set to a gel. Leave to cool.

CHAPTER 7
WEDDING CAKE

Christmas may have been Charles Dickens's most compelling theme, but he was keen on a wedding, too: there are three in *The Pickwick Papers*, which he finished writing at the Doughty Street house. And he created what is probably the most memorable wedding cake in all of English literature: the spider-infested, decaying centrepiece of the wedding feast of poor Miss Havisham in *Great Expectations*.

Most wedding cakes, in life and in art, have much happier associations than that ghastly relic: they represent the happy couple as their status changes, and two become one. As Diane Purkiss points out in her recent book *English Food, A People's History*, cake often appears when change is occurring. The observation is supported by countless images pasted into old photograph albums and resting quietly on smartphones. In the background at that leaving do, on the table at the children's birthday party, on the fancy multi-tiered serving stand in the swanky hotel celebrating the award of a degree or a medal... on display at the christening, the bar mitzvah, the funeral. And of course taking centre stage as the bride and groom plunge the knife into the spectacular creation that shares star billing on their wedding day.

All times of change – of age, or direction, or spiritual growth – celebrate a new presence or a new absence. And always the cake is there, providing not just sustenance but a moment of luxuriance and deliciousness, a slice of comfort, and one of the most ancient demonstrations of fellowship known to mankind: the sharing of good food.

Of all cakes the wedding cake may be the most powerfully symbolic, remaining so even as the institution of marriage itself has changed over the centuries. In my story of cake, it follows Dundee and Christmas cake as the last of the mighty fruit cakes because, as we shall see, unlike those two, wedding cake is changing in the twenty-first century as the traditional style is overtaken – for the moment – by new versions. This edible centrepiece can take many forms, some of them not really cake at all, but it retains a hugely significant role in the proceedings: the Cutting of the Cake will have its own line on the schedule, if not actually printed in the menus for the wedding breakfast then certainly inscribed – and quite possibly underlined – in the wedding planner's timetable.

Every wedding is different, but I have never been to one without a cake, although the guise it takes is often bizarre: ranks of cupcakes, a pyramid of doughnuts, tiers of cheese... and every couple has decisions to make about this element of their big day that may be every bit as contentious as what colour the bridegroom's tie should be, how many bridesmaids should be recruited and whether or not to invite Unreliable Uncle Roger.

The cake decision is not only important in symbolic terms; it may be indecorous to mention it, but there is a cost element as well: a standard two-tier cake can cost around £350, and a three-tier £500; cheese tiers are no cheaper.

As I mentioned in Chapter Three, although I have lived with the same lovely woman for more than a quarter of a century, and although we have raised two gorgeous and precious daughters together, we have never got married.

This is not the moment to explore that particular topic – this is my book about cake, not my autobiography – but it does mean that I can't dip into my own personal experience of a wedding in order to explore matrimonial cake-related issues. My mother wasn't a great deal of use in this regard either: when I asked her what was special about her wedding cake in 1961, she first of all said, 'Nothing,' and then, a little more helpfully, added: 'The fact that it was a cake was special enough. It was fruit cake with royal icing, and all that sugar was a treat in itself. Remember, ten years earlier sugar was still being rationed.'

Not a great deal of valuable insight there.

Luckily, though, I was involved, fairly centrally, in a wedding while I was writing the book, which gave me the opportunity to pick the brains of the bride – and her cake-maker.

The bride was my first cousin Janie, a dear friend as well as a close relative. Her father sadly passed away a few years ago, and Janie accorded me the great honour of giving her away. My daughters have not yet gone in for matrimony, so this was not a role that I had played before, but Janie and her husband-to-be, Graeme, made sure that my part in their nuptials was as undemanding and delightful as possible.

The ceremony took place in a small-scale stately home – technically a cottage orné, if you are familiar with the term – with beautiful gardens overlooking a bend of the River Test in Hampshire. Drinks afterwards were taken in the walled garden and dinner was served in the flower-decked adjoining conservatory.

The entire scenario was planned and executed in the height of good taste, and there was beauty everywhere you looked. Under these circumstances there was a certain amount of pressure on the cake, which sat in majesty on its own table at the head of proceedings, so that all the guests had to process past it to take their seats for dinner.

The cake had been made, not by a caterer, but by the maid of honour, Denise, who – as if she hadn't already had enough to cope with – sat next to me at dinner.

That gave me a tremendous opportunity to grill her about her duties (organising bridesmaids, supervising bride's costume, checking flowers, reassuring bride that all of the above had been done, etc.) and her cake-making. Which, it turned out, had taken place over the same extended timetable as all the other wedding preparations.

Denise, who works in a primary school by day, is well established among her friendship group as an accomplished amateur baker, with a strong line in character-based occasion cakes. Janie might have asked the caterers who provided the rest of the dinner (which was imaginative and accomplished) to do the cake as well, but she had seen Denise's work and liked the idea of keeping it personal.

A bonus was that, unlike a professional baker whose briefing time is necessarily limited, Denise had ample opportunity to discuss possibilities while hanging out with Janie and Graeme in the normal course of their social life. After initial discussions, she asked them both to send her – separately – any ideas they had come across in magazines and on websites that had appealed.

Janie, who had said that she loved Denise's character cakes 'because they told a story', swerved off in another direction and sent her a bunch of pictures of traditional tiered cakes. Graeme stayed true to form and sent photographs of *Star Wars* and Lego cakes.

Eventually the daunting range of likes and dislikes, suggestions and counter-suggestions, not to mention full and frank exchanges of views, were gradually refined into a workable project.

Not that Denise sought to have Janie and Graeme's sign-off on a detailed brief: once she was confident that she had a good sense of what they might be after, she called a halt to the consultation process and just said, Leave it with me.

Like all the other guests, I had spent several minutes admiring the cake from every angle before sitting down to dinner. It was in three tiers, and I was assuming the standard modern triple sponge base. Not so.

'They both love fruit cake, so the bottom tier was always going to be fruit,' Denise explained. 'I didn't let on that I was planning on making a three-tier cake. Janie assumed that I would do a single cake. But I believe every woman deserves at least one three-tier cake during their lifetime, so it had to be three! Knowing that Graeme likes my lemon drizzle cake I decided on lemon sponges for the two top tiers with a lemon and cream-cheese filling.'

Long before those layers were baked, though, construction started on the sugar paste adornments: 'The harder they set, the better,' Denise observed, and I thought of the semi-fossilised decorations from royal wedding cakes displayed in historic palaces.

She made blackberries, because the newlyweds' home is called Brambles; a poppy, for a much loved and now departed cat; walking boots to reflect their daily hikes around the village and beyond; an anchor to represent the many cruises they have enjoyed together; a golden bullet inscribed with 007 for their shared love of James Bond films ('annoying that the franchise decided to kill 007 off between me finishing the sugar work and the wedding day and they came home from the cinema saying that they'd both had it with the films'), and Lego bricks for modelling-mad Graeme.

'Finally, to show how they are still their own people, a signpost with one sign pointing North to the Royal Opera House (Janie's passion), one pointing South to Fratton Park, Portsmouth FC's ground (Graeme's passion) and a third pointing West to Houghton Lodge (the wedding venue).'

Cleverly, Denise confined the storytelling elements to the rear of the cake (not visible from the dinner table), while from the front it appeared a traditional tiered wedding cake. All the sculpted elements, as well as delicate sugarwork flowers which

Denise had made in consultation with Janie's florist, were arranged on a smooth layer of rolled sugar paste for an immaculate yet practical finish.

The three cakes making up the tiers, ribboned in the wedding colours but otherwise unadorned, were covered and transported to the venue the night before the wedding in Denise's car, driven with extreme care along twisting Hampshire lanes, together with two boxes filled with the hand-modelled decorations.

Denise put it all together the night before the wedding: 'It was terrifying, honestly... I had no idea what the finished cake would look like, and I was really worried that it wouldn't match the picture that I had in my head.'

It did – though not without a dreadful moment. 'I dropped a sugar-paste peony which had taken weeks to build and was to be the centrepiece of the top of the cake. It completely shattered into pieces.' Fortunately, and most professionally, Denise had kept the less-than-perfect practice version of the peony – which looked terrific to me – and it was this that sat atop her magnificent creation at the head of the table.

In what seemed to me a stroke of genius, Janie and Graeme had insisted that their reception should focus on fine food rather than dancing, although a brilliant singer and pianist had entertained us all earlier on. Instead of a deafening disco and excruciating middle-aged dance moves, there were seven courses of gently paced and exquisitely presented fine food, after which all the guests gathered admiringly around the cake.

Denise held her breath while bride and groom performed the ritual cut, after which it was portioned out on to plates as a final dessert course. I got a slice of the fruit cake: as a senior member of the wedding, I felt that I should take the traditional path.

I think on reflection that it is fortunate that at the time of the wedding I had yet to conduct my research into wedding cake history and traditions, otherwise my conversation with Denise might have taken a different turn, with me bombarding her with a party mix of supposedly ancient lore, dodgy imported customs and stuff frankly made up in order to shift oddball catering supplies online.

I wouldn't have wanted such an interrogation to get in the way of such an important experience. My search for the True Slice of wedding cake was barely a quest at all: life brought it to me without my seeking it out. To be more precise, a waitress brought it to me as I sat between the maid of honour who had baked it and the bride it honoured. Simply fruit cake and pure white icing. It looked beautiful and tasted delicious, but that is not the point: with a wedding cake, the True Slice is served at the right time, in the right company.

CRUMBS OF KNOWLEDGE
WHY SO MANY FRUIT CAKES?

The base tier of Janie and Graeme's wedding cake was a fruit cake, the traditional form of wedding cake... and the fifth fruit cake, after Eccles, Banbury, Dundee and Christmas cakes, which I have mentioned.

Why are fruit cakes still so popular, and why do they pop up in different contexts in British life?

Any nation's cuisine is bound to be based on the raw materials available, and in Britain there is abundant fruit, from hedgerows and trees: it's inevitable that it would have been used to augment basic recipes from the very earliest days of cooking.

We know from the writings of Apicius that the Romans had a cake or loaf of dried fruit, honey and nuts held together in grain mash, and some version of this will inevitably have travelled with them to Britain – where the residents may well have come up with a similar idea independently.

A descendant of this, raised with yeast but still dense and heavily fruited, became the Great Cake of medieval feast days, direct ancestor of our ubiquitous fruit cakes today. The embellishments that distinguish one from another are merely matters of style and custom: as the great American talk show host Johnny Carson put it: 'There is only one fruit-cake in the entire world, and people keep sending it to each other.'

Why? Because fruit cake is a portable, resilient, reliable store of goodness. It is versatile: it can be iced as a dessert, topped with cheese and served as a main course (in Yorkshire), taken on an Antarctic expedition as a lifesaver. It is democratic: dressed up for a royal wedding, dressed down for a church fête.

> And it keeps: in the right conditions, fruit cake lasts for centuries. While fancier, flimsier cakes decay and disappear, fruit cake will always be with us.

The bride and groom departed on their honeymoon cruise; Denise heaved a sigh of relief. I settled down to look further into the history and practice of wedding cake.

It quickly became clear to me, diving into the reams of material, that any couple who chose to include every cake-related custom they could find in their recipe and order of ceremony would end up with (a) a very odd-looking cake and (b) some very perplexed guests.

What a wedding cake looks like depends not only on the aesthetic impression that the nuptial pair wish to convey, but also what they actually want to do with their cake. Because while most other cakes are also capable of being admired for their looks, they exist primarily to be eaten. Not so a wedding cake, which should certainly be edible, but must possess a number of other qualities.

A selection of traditions, and more recently adopted customs, will underscore some of the choices that need to be made.

First of all, texture and durability. According to many wedding websites, in ancient Rome the cake, or a bread-like confection, was broken over the bride's head as a symbol of good fortune. Guests then scrambled around for the crumbs to share in the luck. Over time this tradition evolved into the sharing – and throwing – of handfuls of dried fruit and sweetened nuts called, in Italian, *confetto*... plural confetti, which is – well, you get the picture.

In the Victorian era, though, it was important that the cake should be less fragile and more durable, as couples were supposed to preserve the top level of a multi-tiered cake intact, so that it could be served at the christening of the first child. The cake therefore needed to be long-lasting, for example a solid fruit cake shored up with a layer of marzipan and sealed with concrete-like royal icing. Try breaking that over the bride's head and she would be knocked unconscious: a poor start to the honeymoon.

That's one choice. Another crucial aspect of the cake is cuttability and what a chef might call portioning concerns. As I have already mentioned, Cutting the Cake is a big moment at every wedding reception, traditionally the first task that the couple undertake together, and symbolic of the hospitality they will offer their friends and family in future. The most important point is that the cake should be cuttable without too much effort on the part of the bride and groom, as they will be simultaneously cutting the cake and posing for the wedding photographer, with the bride's hand uppermost on the knife so that her ring is prominent and catching the light and both of them smiling beatifically – in other words, not really concentrating on what they are doing.

If the icing is too solid, the knife will bounce off and/or there may be a horrible accident. But if the cake is too soft or the icing too thin, it will be a nightmare to cut and portion rapidly and efficiently for all the guests.

Before that happens, there may be one other intimate cake-related moment where the couple's choices may have some bearing on events. After cutting the cake to whoops and cheers, many couples choose to share the first slice with each other, usually interlinking their forearms in a manoeuvre worthy of experienced Scottish reelers.

For the cake-sharing to come off, the cake must be solid enough to maintain its structural integrity while they fiddle around with their arms and hands and the photographer adjusts his angles. So a firm-textured cake is a good thing here, but not so good if the couple follow up with the increasingly popular and tremendously messy recent custom of mashing the cake into each other's faces, causing inevitable damage to décolletage, morning suit, dignity, etc. General food fights can ensue at this point, depending on previous alcohol consumption, which can be very upsetting, not least for the cake-maker. I blame the Americans.

I'm not going to go into all the wedding cake traditions and their implications in similar detail, but I leave you with one that requires a different kind of durability from the cake: this is the notion that 'maiden ladies' attending the wedding take with them afterwards a morsel of cake which they place under their pillow that night, or (racier and messier accounts suggest) place in their stocking overnight, so that they are bound to dream of their future husband – or, since even ancient traditions may be updated, wife.

CRUMBS OF KNOWLEDGE
LETHAL CUSTOMS

Ammunition for a nuptial food fight is one unusual employment for wedding cake: lethal weapon is another. In *After the Funeral*, an Hercule Poirot murder mystery by Agatha Christie, one of the characters is poisoned by a slice of wedding cake that has been laced with arsenic and then posted through her letterbox in a little presentation parcel. This custom, common in my youth, is dying out as caterers turn to less hefty – and thus less postable – forms of cake. But it's not dying out as rapidly as Christie's characters do.

The individual with the most responsibility for what is thought of as the traditional British wedding cake, the tall, multi-tiered architectural extravaganza, is Queen Victoria, who keeps cropping up in our national cake story (see also Queen Victoria's sandwich and Battenberg cake).

The Queen Empress did not court publicity, but she reigned in an age when mass-circulation newspapers and periodicals were not only booming but were – crucially – lavishly illustrated, often in colour and in great detail.

The royal family and their doings provided wonderful raw material for the artists, with the result that their pastimes, fashions and what might be called lifestyle accoutrements were seen – and copied – by millions of Her Majesty's subjects.

The cake produced for Victoria and Albert's wedding in 1840 was a spectacular case in point. Like many aspects of Victoria's home life, it was conceived on a grand scale and in questionable taste, and had artistic pretensions and a decidedly sentimental character.

The vast construction weighed 300 pounds and measured three yards in circumference. It was officially described as 'ponderous and elegant', and the first of those terms was certainly true. Mr Mawditt, the Yeoman Confectioner to Her Majesty, surmounted a vast disc of iced fruit cake more than a foot deep with three further tiers supporting classically draped sugarwork statuettes representing Britannia blessing the illustrious Bride and Bridegroom. At the feet of the leading characters sat a dog, representing fidelity, implausibly ignoring two turtle doves, representing felicity, while a number of plump cupids, dressed in order to avoid indecorum, danced attendance with national emblems of one kind and another. The base was ornamented with swags of orange blossom and myrtle and the overwhelming impression is of mawkishness and dazzling white royal icing, both in staggering proportions.

As well as size, incidentally, the cake had staying power. A slice in its original presentation box was sold at auction in 2016 for £1,500.

Few of Victoria's subjects could afford to mimic the scale or even the style of Her Majesty's matrimonial monster, but the notion of sculpted figures of bride and groom surmounting the cake did catch on quickly.

The extra height of Queen Victoria's cake was likely to have been influenced by tall cakes popular in France in the early nineteenth century, and did not really take flight in Britain until later in that century, when falling sugar prices allowed for greater extravagance on the part of wedding caterers.

Another force driving wedding cakes to ever greater heights was not Queen Victoria but her ever-burgeoning family, every detail of whose nuptials was examined by the media with a fervour that seems very familiar these days.

When, for example, Victoria's eldest child, also called Victoria, married Prince Frederick William of Prussia in 1858, her cake sported three layers of columns and the edifice was six feet tall. When Queen Victoria's grandson, later King George V, married Princess Mary of Teck in 1893 he upped the ante further: twelve inches further, in fact. And the royal race to the sky did not end there. When Queen Victoria's great-grandson, the future King George VI, married Lady Elizabeth Bowes-Lyon (known as the Queen Mother for much of the twentieth century), their cake had no fewer than nine tiers and was ten feet tall.

Since then, royal wedding cakes have declined in height, which social commentators may choose to see as a metaphor for the fortunes of the nation, but I see more as a matter of physics, engineering and health and safety regulations. Princess Elizabeth marries Prince Philip of Greece, 1947: 9ft. Prince Charles and Lady Diana Spencer, 1981: 5ft. Prince William and Catherine Middleton, 2011: 3ft (but eight tiers and about 2ft 6in wide – minimal risk of collapse on big-name guests and subsequent lawsuits).

Before we move on from tiers and toffs to buttercreamed slabs and the wider public, a word on the creation myth of all tiered wedding cakes: the notion that they were all inspired by St Bride's in Fleet Street and its wonderful tiered spire.

This beautiful church – the spiritual home of journalists, if my benighted trade can be said to have any such thing – was designed by Christopher Wren and opened in 1675, though the spire, which is Wren's tallest, was not finished until 1703.

Numerous London guidebooks and websites will tell you that some time in the eighteenth century an apprentice baker called William Rich, who worked on Ludgate Hill just to the east, fell in love with his boss's daughter, and either made an elaborate cake to prove himself worthy of her hand, or won her hand and made the cake for the wedding; or that Rich was a baker and made a cake based on the church's spire for his daughter's wedding, which is less romantic and therefore more plausible.

As far as I can discover there is no written evidence for any of these tales, and the whole story may have a lot to do with the appearance of the steeple and the name of the church – which is nothing to do with weddings and a lot to do with the saint it was named after many centuries ago, who is also known as St Brigid.

There.

Like so much else to do with weddings, the eventual cake, and what is done to it, are the sum of a series of choices made by the couple-to-be from a smorgasbord of options that may be influenced by their families, their cultural inheritance, their friends, their dating history and – increasingly likely these days – some crazy stuff that someone shared with them off TikTok.

To get an idea of how a professional deals with such demands, I had tea – and cake – with Lucy Netherton, whose beautiful creations are much in demand among the marrying couples of south-east England. 'The cake is a big statement,' Lucy said. 'The photograph of the bride and groom cutting the cake is likely to be something that they treasure and share for years, so it's got to be just right.'

Style counts at least as much as substance, and the wedding cake maker has to follow the couple's aesthetic wishes – or those of their wedding planner. 'Some people are pretty laid back, and just give me a colour cue from the bridesmaid's dresses, or the buttonhole flowers of the ushers,' Lucy told me. 'Others are more specific – they might want a sugarwork model of their dog, say, or a Disney theme.'

Working with a wedding planner can cut both ways: on the one hand, they can be demanding and interpose an additional layer of communication between cake-maker and customer; on the other, they often know the venue and can provide valuable logistical support on the day, for instance by providing rapid protection from the elements.

As well as fulfilling the visual fantasies of their clients, wedding cake makers also have to be supremely technically competent – and pragmatic. Although the visible architectural elements of the Victorian cake are no longer in demand, the smooth-sided buttercream sponge which is all the rage these days still has structural issues which the diligent baker must address.

CAKE

'It's got to stand up straight,' as Lucy pointed out, 'and it may have to stand up straight for some time.' At the very least, the cake has to be admired by guests on the way into the reception, and then survive through the reception as far as the vital first cut – after which it is likely to be spirited away to be portioned by the caterers, either into little boxes to be taken away by the guests when they leave (a hangover from Victorian traditions not well suited to modern cakes) or, more sensibly, on to plates to be served as part of the dessert course.

All of this takes time, and since most weddings take place in the summer, and often in outdoor marquees, or hotel reception rooms without air conditioning, the cake must be durable.

'You have to manage people's expectations a little,' Lucy said. No cake constructed of sponge and buttercream will still look its best after several hours on a table in a heatwave. That's physics and chemistry. Lucy tries to ensure that her cakes spend a relatively short time on display before cutting – or she intervenes.

'One couple wanted all their guests to see the cake on their way into the ceremony, and then of course have it on display at the reception several hours later. I dismantled it and took it home to my fridge while they were actually getting married, then rebuilt it later.'

That is the kind of practical engineering skill – and problem-solving attitude – that any successful wedding cake maker needs to survive and thrive in a competitive industry. Look at Lucy's Instagram feed (@bybbakery – a key source of custom for her) and you see witty, pretty concepts immaculately executed. What you don't see are the underpinnings, the kit and the tactics required to bring them to fruition.

To bake a successful cake you need little more than the ability to combine ingredients, switch on an oven and (later) splat on some buttercream. To make and display a successful wedding cake you are also likely to need dowel rods, separator plates, a spirit level – and a car with a generous passenger footwell.

'I always transport cakes on the floor of my car,' Lucy explained. It's out of the sun, it's level, and it's low down, close to the car's centre of gravity. 'We don't want tipping,' she gravely observed.

Nor does one want buttercream-slide, a risk in hot weather which can be warded off – to some extent – by stiffening the mixture, but is best prevented, like many of the ills a wedding cake is prey to, by delicately guiding the choices which the happy-couple-to-be make.

The commonplace contemporary combo of sponge 'n' buttercream doesn't keep on display in hot weather, and neither does it survive for long in little boxes as a guests' keepsake.

I have seen portions of cake in museums from weddings that took place decades ago, still visually intact and – in extremis – probably still edible. But if you keep a slice of sponge in its box for even a couple of days, what you will have is some sweet slime and a soggy box.

You could, if you wished, see this as evidence of our live-for-the-day throwaway consumer society, all style and no substance. Or you could, like Lucy Netherton, see it as a passing trend, the latest turn of the eternally spinning wheel of fashion.

'I've been making wedding cakes for years, and I've never been asked to make a fruit cake with royal icing,' Lucy told me. 'I'd love to do it, and I'd love the challenge of making a tier of the cake that would still be delicious when served at a christening a year later.' But no one, at present, is asking for such creations.

'That style of cake will come back one day soon, I'm absolutely sure of it,' Lucy said. 'It only takes a celebrity, or a princess, to take that route, and it will catch on again. I'll be ready.'

Perhaps I'll get married one day, though the decision clearly won't be mine alone. If I do I'll be colossally well-informed about wedding cakes, and able to share my vast learning and informed opinions with my bride-to-be... what? Not such a good idea? Keep it to myself? Yes. Probably for the best.

That particular True Slice may lie in the future.

A TWENTY-FIRST-CENTURY WEDDING CAKE

It's not difficult to find recipes for a classic wedding cake, so instead I wanted to include a thoroughly up-to-date version. Of course, all wedding cakes are personal – and this was Lucy Netherton's recipe for her own wedding.

Lucy noted: 'Wedding cakes can often cost a lot of money – and rightly so, as they take lots of time, patience and love to create. This cake is perfect if you're trying to keep the costs down, as it's a really simple design that you'll need very little special equipment for. Don't even worry if your icing isn't perfectly smooth: it should look home-made because it is – it's made with love! The fruit and flowers help to finish this cake perfectly and give it an elegant and stylish finish.'

You will need two cake boards just slightly larger than your tins and a strong cake lifter; these are not expensive and are easy to find online.

SERVES 60

CAKE

Red velvet layer

425g unsalted butter, very soft

425g light brown soft sugar

red food colouring paste (I used Sugarflair Red Extra paste)

7 large eggs, beaten

375g self-raising flour

75g cocoa powder

8 tbsp buttermilk

1 tsp white wine vinegar

1 tsp bicarbonate of soda

Cheesecake layer

1.35kg full-fat cream cheese

450g caster sugar

6 tbsp plain flour

1 tbsp vanilla bean paste

450ml sour cream or crème fraîche

6 large eggs

Buttercream

1.25kg unsalted butter, very soft

2.5kg icing sugar

about 6 tbsp milk

1 tbsp vanilla bean paste

To decorate

a selection of berries and flowers (gypsophila, roses and
peonies all work really well)

WEDDING CAKE

1. Preheat the oven to 170°C/325°F/Gas Mark 3. Grease and line the bases of two 18cm springform tins and two 23cm springform tins.

2. Make the cheesecake layer first. Put all the ingredients into a really big bowl, then beat with electric mixers until smooth, 1–2 minutes.

3. Divide between the four prepared tins: if you weigh the amounts the layers will be more even. You need about 550g in each of the small tins and 750g in each of the big tins.

4. Bake for 50 minutes, then check: they should be set with a slight wobble in the centre; bake for 5 minutes more if they aren't quite set enough. Remove and leave to cool completely in the tins before carefully removing and transferring to a flat plate or board in the fridge until you need them.

5. Preheat the oven to 180°C/350°F/Gas Mark 4. Once you've washed your tins you can re-line them with parchment and grease them well again, ready for the red velvet cake layer. Beat the soft butter and sugar until really fluffy, a couple of minutes. Add your red colouring paste, a little at a time – I use a cocktail stick. You want a really vivid red colour. Add the eggs, little by little, beating well after each addition.

6. Fold in the flour, cocoa, buttermilk, vinegar and bicarb with a large metal spoon until well combined and no floury patches remain. Check the colour; add a little more food colouring paste if you need to.

7. Divide between the four prepared tins: if you weigh the amounts it will be more even. You need about 375g in each of the small tins and 550g in each of the big tins.

8. Cook for 22–30 minutes (the smaller cakes may be done after 22, the larger slightly longer) until risen and springy to the touch. Check with a skewer – it should come out clean. Remove and leave to cool completely in the tins before carefully removing. If not icing straight away, wrap the cakes in clingfilm until you need them.

9. Make the buttercream: mash the butter and icing sugar together in a large bowl; this will stop your kitchen being sprayed with a cloud of icing sugar. Once mashed, beat with an electric mixer until pale and fluffy. Add the milk and vanilla and beat for about 45 seconds more.

10. You may want to use a cake turntable to help you ice the cake – it certainly makes it easier to spin the cake around and ice it evenly all over.

11. Take your large cake board and add a little blob of buttercream to help the cake stick to the board. Start with a red velvet sponge, and cover it with buttercream, spreading it out with a palette knife; then top with your first cheesecake layer, cover with more buttercream; then another then red velvet layer, more buttercream, and lastly the final cheesecake layer.

12. Next use a palette knife to roughly cover the entire cake with a thin layer of buttercream. Don't worry too

much about the appearance at this stage – this is called a crumb coat and ensures that your final layer is crumb-free. Chill the cake for at least 30 minutes to firm up the icing. Use a cake lifter to transfer it to the fridge. Repeat with the smaller cake.

13. Once the first coat of the icing is chilled, use the remaining icing to completely cover the cakes again. This is easiest if you pile the icing on top of the cake, and then use a palette knife to ease it over the edge and down the sides. Chill both for another 30 minutes or overnight at this stage if you would like.

14. Using a cake lifter, carefully lift your cake and its board on to your stand (make sure the stand you choose has room for fruit decoration around the edge, as well as the cake). Carefully lift the other cake, using your lifter, and place it in the centre of the bottom layer. Pile your fruit and flowers on top. Dust with icing sugar just before presenting the cake.

15. Get ahead. I assembled my cake at about 11am on the big day; it was then kept in a cool place until we cut it at 10pm – so it would hold. I made the cheesecakes two days in advance and the sponge one day in advance. Then I iced each layer the night before and kept them in the fridge.

CHAPTER 8
GINGER CAKE

As noted above, one of the most magnificent wedding cakes of the Victorian era was that constructed to celebrate the nuptials of the future King George V and Queen Mary, in 1893. It was seen – in person – by more than 14,000 people, and no doubt provided marvellous publicity for the firm which had made it, McVitie & Price of Edinburgh.

These days the company survives as plain McVitie's, but I remember one of their cakes well from my childhood, though it was a much smaller – and no doubt stickier – confection than the royal centrepiece. And that cake of my youth still exists.

Purely in the interests of research, I was browsing the cake aisle in my local supermarket the other day and my eye was caught by a wrapper that took me back instantly more than half a century. It read: McVitie's Jamaica Ginger, and it took me – somewhat against my will – to my Great Aunt Ada's sitting room.

Great Aunt Ada lived in Barkingside, in the far east of London. She was my father's father's sister, a retired teacher with a somewhat abrupt manner. She was of good height but stooped by age (in her eighties, as I recall her); she wore severe spectacles which magnified the size of her milky blue eyes, and in one ear she wore an enormous hearing aid, which whistled from time to time until she flicked it with a finger to shut it up. As a child I had the strong impression that she might also extend the flicking finger to a noisy great-nephew if provoked; my brother agreed and we were always on our best behaviour on our rare visits to her house.

It wouldn't be fair to characterise G. A. Ada as fierce, though: she was simply dignified, and expected politeness, and when she was shown it she would produce rewards, such as R. Whites lemonade in its patterned clear-glass bottle, the most grown-up form of fizzy drink it was possible to imagine; and McVitie's Jamaica Ginger cake, which came in a serrated paper cradle.

I remember that when Great Aunt Ada peeled back the fluted paper it stuck to the cake within, as if reluctant to let go, and I remember that the cake squished as she pushed the slicer through it, so that what arrived on my plate was not a rectangle but a squashed rectangle – later on I'd know it as a parallelogram.

It seemed an adult cake: the minuscule amount of ginger it contained was certainly the first spice that my cosseted Anglo-Saxon palate ever encountered. I thought it was thrilling, and made polite noises about it until I was offered some more. It was a proper treat – yet not enough to make me love Great Aunt Ada.

Perhaps it was the austere environment: G. A. Ada lived alone, surrounded in her neat little house by giant brown furniture inherited from her parents. We sat on tall, hard chairs around a monolithic oaken table. Glass-fronted cabinets held little china and glass animals: intriguing, but clearly not to be touched. There were antimacassars on the armchairs and doilies everywhere; the tea-set was elaborate, with pretty china and complex silver implements.

I have a lingering sense of fear about visiting Great Aunt Ada – not because she was ever unkind in any way; it was just that I always felt that small boys were surplus to requirements in her house, that she didn't know what to do with us and that we didn't know what to do with ourselves when on her premises... and I was always frightened of dropping a precious plate, or smearing ginger cake goo on a doily or some similar crime.

Still, the memory of the cake stayed with me, long after Great Aunt Ada passed away (in her late nineties), bequeathing us the vast oval table, on which as teenagers my brother and I played war games, and one of her glass-fronted cabinets, which we filled with toy racing cars.

She also bequeathed to me a fondness for McVitie's Jamaica Ginger, so when I saw it in the supermarket I scooped it up and brought it home, keen to see what sensations it might provoke.

It certainly prompted memories (see above), though not culinary ecstasy. McVitie's may be justly celebrated for their Digestive biscuits, but they are no slouch in the cake department. They invented (in 1927) the Jaffa Cake – subsequently proved a cake, not a biscuit, in the courts – and made not only George and Mary's royal wedding cake, but that of the future Queen Elizabeth II and Prince Philip.

Their Jamaica Ginger cake is not so legally or historically significant, but it is – as my memories suggest – a solidly twentieth-century invention, which is why it sits here in the book, between the fruit cakes and other, more recent innovations.

It's not very gingery, though. It may be that my palate has been dulled by years of powerful curries and chilli-based table sauces, but I didn't feel any kind of kick from the cake. I wasn't greatly surprised, therefore, to look at the ingredients on the pack and find that 'ginger flavouring' is absolutely last on the list.

All the same, it kick-started my mind. I wondered first if there was real ginger involved in the ginger flavouring, then if it really came from Jamaica... because, it suddenly occurred to me, it's not the cake that's Jamaican, necessarily, it's the ginger, and food marketing being what it is, perhaps not even that.

And perhaps it was the stern schoolmistress shade of Great Aunt Ada wagging a finger at me, but these thoughts prompted more, not just about ginger and Jamaica but about spice, and sugar, and Britain, and cake.

I resolved to try and get that big, important story straight, because it doesn't seem right to tell the story of cake and this country without acknowledging the part that the sugar trade and the spice trade and all their dreadful heritage played. And in the process it seemed a good idea also to look for an authentic Jamaican ginger cake, if that turned out to be appropriate. Or even existent.

So, to recap: cake evolved in this country when cookery was basic, and oats were bound with fat of some kind, probably lard or butter, and flavoured if possible with fruit or honey before being cooked in the embers of the hearth or burnt by careless monarchs.

Later on exciting stuff like currants arrived from the Middle East, along with spices for the very wealthy, to add excitement to cakes that were enjoyed on religious feast days.

Sugar was rare and very expensive for centuries, and only became cheaper and much more widely available through the widespread practice of slavery in the colonies where it was grown. The increase in consumption was startling: consumption of sugar per capita in Britain was 4lb in 1704, 18lb in 1800 and 90lb in 1901. Clearly a lot of that went into cups of tea and pots of jam, but a vast amount, by the middle of the nineteenth century, was going into mass-manufactured cakes.

Slavery was abolished before the end of the nineteenth century, but the employment of cheap and indentured labour was not, and the question: 'How sure are you that the sugar you are using is ethically produced?' is still very much worth asking today.

I'm not suggesting that cake is evil or that we should feel bad about eating it, but I do think it's appropriate to acknowledge how its rise to such popularity came about.

I also think it's a good idea to celebrate some of the great stuff that has come our way from the Caribbean in less sinister ways, and one of the best places to do that in the UK is in Brixton in south London, home to many excellent bakeries and also, I hoped, to a gingery cake that might be truer to the spice and to the cuisine of the island that it comes from.

I love Brixton. It's a brilliant mix of all the things that make London such a terrific city, and which have been tidied up to an excessive extent elsewhere in the metropolis.

The shops are fantastic, especially off the main drag, on Electric Avenue and Atlantic Road: no slick chains, but busy emporia crammed with fascinating stuff: fresh food, great music, wild clothing.

I often pop down for half an hour at lunchtime just to wander around, so I knew where to go in my search for an authentic ginger cake: First Choice Bakers, facing the elevated railway line on Atlantic Road.

None of your fancy artisanal stuff here: the sign above the battered, much graffitied awning announces that they are 'Producers and suppliers of the finest quality Jamaican Patties, English and Caribbean breads, Buns, Confectionery and other Specialities, i.e. Duck Bread, Cocktail Patties, Takeaway Dinners etc' and all that is no word of a lie.

Every time I have been in or been past, there has been a line to get served, reinforced by notices to the effect that no matter what you're buying, you have to queue to get it.

On the plain white wooden shelves are stacked wrapped loaves of Mongoose Bread, Hi-Top Bread and loaf-sized brown buns. In the hot cabinet are fresh patties and stuffed rolls: beef, saltfish, fried snapper, jerk chicken.

Unusually for a Brixton food emporium, there is no reggae from powerful speakers, but it's hardly quiet: a constant stream of customers with varied demands makes sure of that. On the afternoon I visited on my cake quest, the remarkably mild-mannered guy behind the counter was dealing simultaneously with a woman who wanted four, no five – hell, six – beef patties, a man who wanted a Hi-Top loaf and a round bun in two separate bags and a lady who had brought her bicycle into the shop and who didn't want to buy anything, but did want change for a £20 note.

'What do you need?' he asked, turning to me, having sorted all three with speed and good grace. Jamaican ginger cake, I said.

'No such thing,' he said, with friendly firmness. That stuff in the supermarket, he suggested, that's not Jamaican cake. That's English cake.

Right. I get it. Hastily, aware of the queue behind me, I said: 'OK, is there a Jamaican cake that is made with ginger?'

'Sure! You need a bulla cake. Here.' He whisked a cellophaned package off the shelf and on to the counter. 'It's beautiful. Full of ginger spice. Enjoy.'

I paid him and left, feeling an odd mixture of humiliation and exhilaration.

It was beautiful indeed, when I tried it at home, but it was more a bread flavoured with ginger than a cake.

Perhaps the man in the bakery was right, and the notion of Jamaican ginger cake was nothing more than a marketing ploy. I needed confirmation. I bought a copy of an excellent new book about Jamaican cuisine, *Motherland*, by Melissa Thompson. No ginger cake. No bulla either. But a mouth-watering recipe for the rich, spiced, fruited loaf called bun, which is often eaten with cheese. The author, raised in Dorset, descends from Jamaican bakers, and explains in her book that Jamaican bun is properly eaten with the island's bright orange Tastee cheese, suggesting Red Leicester as an acceptable substitute for British consumers.

All very interesting, and very tasty, and certainly a cake that has become part of British life by way of the Jamaican-heritage community – but is bun ever made with ginger, and is it any relation to Jamaica ginger cake?

'No,' said Thompson when I rang her up to ask. It might have been a very short conversation. But, she kindly added, she remembered McVitie's Jamaica Ginger cake from her own childhood: 'So sticky! And that paper wrapper. I remember the cake always stuck to the paper so that when the cake was finished you could scrape the paper – I did this! – and roll the bits of cake that had been sticking to the paper into a ball, and eat that.'

But, she told me, 'I don't think there's anything very Jamaican about that cake – I think they just chose the word "Jamaica" because it sounded exotic. There isn't an actual Jamaican cake I know that is like that.'

And there isn't even anything essentially Jamaican about ginger, which is a plant native to Asia, not the Caribbean. So Great Aunt Ada's cake, like Mr Kipling's un-Gallic French Fancies – and indeed Mr Kipling himself – has a lot more to do with marketing than authenticity.

I had to accept that the search for a proper British/Jamaican ginger cake had been misguided, skewed by my childhood memories. But cakes flavoured with ginger remain a stalwart in British life, so maybe it would be simpler to look instead for a British ginger cake. And the best place to find that, I reckoned, was Yorkshire.

Parkin, as anyone from that vast and hungry county will tell you, is just the stuff to keep out the cold on Bonfire Night. Purists hold that this dense and filling confection of oats, treacle and ginger should not be consumed earlier in the year than the first week of November, but happily for the rest of us it is commonly available all the year round.

It's easy to find parkin all over Yorkshire (and, whisper it, in Lancashire too); in the past I've enjoyed an honest slice – or chunk – in Botham's of Whitby, watching the Goths parade around the town where Dracula, according to Bram Stoker, came ashore. But that's a long day's journey from the South, and as chance would have it I was due in York to visit the chocolate museum there; and York has a branch of Bettys.

There are those – Yorkshire folk among them – who find Bettys a bit twee, who allege that there is more than a hint of the theme park about the Edwardian decor and the monochrome uniforms of the waiting staff. Such carpers cite the cameo appearance of the shop in Downton Abbey as evidence that the whole set-up is some kind of parody. But I'm not listening. I love Bettys – they dropped the apostrophe years ago – the elegance, the friendliness and the darn good cakes.

The York branch has been serving teas in a setting reminiscent of the interior of a grand ocean liner since the 1930s, and

I was very happy to settle there on a cold, damp morning for a reviving cup of Bettys own blend tea and a slab of parkin from a straw-filled basket of them on the counter.

It's a hefty, straightforward cake, which goes back a good while: Bettys say that the first mention of it by name can be found in court records from 1728, where one Anne Whittaker was accused of stealing oatmeal to make it. That oatmeal is a crucial geographical marker. As the food historian Regula Ysewijn has pointed out, hundreds of years ago bakers used oats in the North, and wheat in the South.

With treacle and golden syrup as well as sugar in the recipe, parkin is never going to win any health awards: but this is a cake, not a staple, something to bring people together on a cold day and energise them. As I munched on my slice I enjoyed the happy background babble of the surrounding tables; not many tourists at this time of year, plenty of confident Yorkshire voices. A different crowd from the Atlantic bakery, but brought together, like Brixton's shoppers, by a love of good, honest baked goods.

I'm not a Yorkshireman, so I may not be the best judge of a True Slice of parkin – this one really hit the spot, though. And no doubt there are better candidates to authenticate the bun and bulla of Brixton. But they are all true parts of the blended national bakery shelf of Britain – and true to those who love them.

At the recent Coronation we had a neighbourhood street party, and friends from all over the country shared images and notes from the similar bashes that they attended. Big, brash, home-made cakes were everywhere to be seen, and I noticed that the bakers all loved sharing what they had made and sampling the efforts of others, all the while comparing notes, discovering new ingredients and flavours and methods.

I'm not going to labour the metaphor, but cake on these occasions provides a means for the many different constituent communities that make up the nation to come together and share a slice of their lives with others. It's a beautiful thing.

YORKSHIRE PARKIN

_____

This recipe, from the time-honoured Yorkshire tea-house empire of Bettys, is for mini-parkins, such as those often served on Bonfire Night – and excellent for a street party. For a single loaf cake, just use a loaf tin and increase the cooking time a little. Whenever I go to Yorkshire I make a point of a cuppa and a piece of cake at a branch of Bettys: they know their stuff.

MAKES 8 MINI-PARKIN LOAVES

100g butter

40g black treacle

180g golden syrup

110g soft brown sugar

100g self-raising flour

3 tsp ground ginger

1 tsp grated nutmeg

40g oats

40g ground almonds

2 tsp whole milk

2 medium eggs

GINGER CAKE

1. Preheat the oven to 180°C/350°F/Gas Mark 4. Line the base of 8 mini-loaf tins with a piece of parchment paper.

2. Place the butter, black treacle, golden syrup and soft brown sugar in a heavy-based pan over a medium heat. Gently warm through to melt the butter and stir until the sugar has completely dissolved. When the mixture comes up to the boil, turn off the heat and set aside while you prepare the other ingredients.

3. In a large mixing bowl, mix together the self-raising flour, spices, oats and ground almonds until they are well combined.

4. Pour the warm mixture over the dry ingredients and mix in well. Set the mixture aside to cool a little.

5. Beat the milk and eggs together thoroughly and then gradually stir into the warm mixture.

6. Pour the mix into the prepared loaf tins and bake in the preheated oven for 20–25 minutes, or until well risen and a skewer inserted into the centre comes out clean.

7. Leave the loaves to cool down slightly before turning out on to a wire cooling rack.

CHAPTER 9
CUPCAKES

Here we leave the cakes that played a big part in the historic life of Britain behind, and enter the territory of the contemporary cake. From this point on, we are in the glorious present. There will still be references to history, though, because the cakes of the past are always with us.

Cakes are not like monarchs: the old does not have to die for the new to be crowned, and tradition lives on alongside innovation. In Manchester, Eccles cakes that would have been recognisable to a medieval merry-maker share a shelf with Pokemon-monster cakes that would send the ancient peasant running for the hills. The latest *Bake-Off*-inspired trends will be on supermarket shelves before Christmas this year; but so will fruit cakes that would have been at home on the table of a Tudor great hall.

All the great cakes of our past live on in the present; some modernised and commercialised, many baked, as they always have been, in domestic kitchens to family recipes. And cakes evolve, not by eradicating the competition, but concurrently, so that in Britain we can embrace, enjoy and eventually adopt cakes from elsewhere without giving up our old favourites.

Enough analysis. Shall we take a little break, to gather our forces? Perhaps with just a tiny twentieth-century sugary snack, one of those ideas from abroad that we have embraced?

A little chapter about cupcakes, then, to restore energy levels.

No objections! You may say that a cupcake is American, and has no place in a book about British cakes. I say 'Phooey': I refer you to my mission statement about the cake as part of British life, and assert that the cupcake clearly qualifies, since (a) a cupcake is just a fairy cake with ideas above its station, and we have all made fairy cakes in our youth, and (b) they are all around us, on every high street.

For instance, it was no trouble at all to get hold of the fuel for this diversion. My office is within a decorative blueberry's throw of three accomplished purveyors of these little beauties: Lola's, Hummingbird and Peggy Porschen. All three of these operators, now with multiple outlets, sprang up in the first decade of this century, riding a wave of enthusiasm for the cakelets that seems to have had very little to do with cookery and a lot to do with sex – or at least *Sex and the City*.

It was... hang on. At this point I needed to run to Lola's, which I achieved with barely a moment exposed to the elements of London. I simply trundled down the vast escalator to the exit from my office building, out of the revolving doors, into the adjacent mainline station by the entrance two metres to the left of our doorway, and up the first escalator on the right.

At the top there is a Lola's... outlet. I think that is the right word, for it is not a shop, or restaurant, or boutique, but simply three chiller cabinets set into the wall of the shopping centre, with a till. The whole thing folds away at night. Think of it as a kind of cupcake wardrobe, and you won't be far off.

Right. Sorted. Vanilla with pink frosting, a close approximation of the cupcake – from New York's Magnolia Bakery – that the character Carrie Bradshaw consumed with obvious enjoyment in an episode of *Sex and the City* that first aired in 2000... a moment that is widely credited with initiating a wave of cupcake mania that – as is often the way with these things – swept first over the United States before washing ashore in the UK.

Very nice it was too, except... I'm not going to be too hard on cupcakes. What would be the point? Unless made by an idiot or a sadist (and there are some flavour combos out there that make me wonder), a cupcake is a pleasing and unchallenging few mouthfuls, not a life-changing event.

Good as far as it goes, which in my case is mostly up my nose. That is my one recurring irritation with these items: I never know how to tackle them. Cupcake vendors are good at providing eggbox-style containers to prevent them flying everywhere in transit, but they tend not to issue you with any kit to aid in the eating process.

If eating at my desk, as I was in the preparation of this chapter, I don't have plates, knives, forks, spoons, etc. to hand. Nor, thankfully, do I have witnesses. So I can take the direct approach, the enthusiast's giant bite, trying to secure in one mouthful equal, and substantial, amounts of cake and topping... with the inevitable result that I get a sizeable injection of pink vanilla buttercream up both nostrils.

It's not for me to say, but I suspect that, as a look, this is far from sexy.

But how else am I supposed to go about it? I suppose I could have licked all, or most, of the buttercream frosting off first, but that seems vulgar, borderline illegal and vaguely sick-making, like eating icing straight from the bowl.

Or go back down to the station and swipe some of that horrible but ethically acceptable wooden cutlery from M&S and attack the cupcake with that... thus making a meal of what is supposed to be no more than a snack. What would Carrie Bradshaw do? Actually, what did Carrie Bradshaw do?

Twenty-five seconds with YouTube later, I can confirm that Carrie employed the same technique as me but had a lot less frosting to deal with, thus leaving her delicate nostrils unencumbered. The same scene now would be a much greater challenge, though I'm sure Sarah Jessica Parker would be up to it.

That moment – it's easy to find the clip – spawned not only a billion-dollar industry, but university theses and a bestselling book (*The Tastemakers: Why We're Crazy for Cupcakes*, by David Sax). And British chains, to return to what I was thinking about before my cake break, were part of the boom.

At the time of writing this sentence, Lola's had made 16,381,904 cupcakes since the company's foundation by two friends, Victoria Jossel and Romy Lewis, in 2006. Oh – now they've made 16,381,905. They have around twenty-five locations in London, including their cupcake closet in Victoria. 16,381,906. Anyway, a lot.

Their cupcakes are nice. I mean, I can't remember coming across one that I actively disliked – the unicorn-themed items are simply irritating – though picking a favourite is oddly difficult. Under pressure from a cupcake-curious interrogator, I would go for the chocolatey one with the sort of coconutty topping, called, I believe, coconut.

As for truth and historical accuracy and the most appropriate spot in which to eat it –well, how about my desk? At and around this workspace I have consumed many Lola's cupcakes, since they are whistled up at the slightest excuse for a workplace festivity, especially if we can't get hold of a Colin the Caterpillar (he'll slither into view soon, I promise).

I've eaten plenty of cupcakes elsewhere: in childhood, when, as I've said, they were known as fairy cakes, and were actually just tiny sponge cakes, thinly iced and sprinkled with hundreds and thousands and handed out for tea after a kickabout in a friend's garden, if he had a diligent mother. And at university, where friends who baked chopped the tops off, cut these lids in half and jammed them into a layer of buttercream and called the result butterfly cakes. This was slightly impressive, but only because it was long before the *Bake Off* raised everyone's expectations.

And then there was *Sex and the City*, and suddenly cupcakes were everywhere, and those who weren't baking them were buying them... from Lola's, or...

I am running out of energy. Time for a Hummingbird. Back in a moment. Bear with – it's a little bit further away than

Lola's cupboard, but still hardly counts as an expedition. Back in a mo.

There we are. I got red velvet, because that's widely said to be the most popular kind of cupcake in the UK – it is certainly the all-time favourite with Hummingbird's customers – and because it gives me a chance to pay my respects to a cake that is unquestionably American, but which has become hugely popular with the British public, not only as a cupcake but as a celebration cake, in chocolate bar form and even, I noticed in Waitrose last weekend, as red velvet granola. It is a brash, challenging kind of cake, beetroot-red sponge topped with a pompadour quiff of cream cheese frosting, and rather a guilty secret of mine – and millions of my compatriots.

My only objection – a grouse common, you will notice, to all my cupcake experiments – is that there is far too much frosting, leading inevitably to involuntary nasal ingestion. And when a key ingredient in the frosting is cream cheese, that's just unacceptable. Who puts cheese up their nose for fun?

Seen from the side – and there weren't many people in the office on the day I was writing this, which allowed for this kind of close inspection – this Hummingbird red velvet cupcake was, in vertical terms, 50% cake (deep red vanilla sponge, with a faint additional aroma of chocolate) and 50% frosting (butter, icing sugar and cream cheese). Too much! If Carrie Bradshaw had tried to take a bite out of this she'd have needed a shower before she could complete the scene.

I finished it anyway, to cover the time I needed to consider the Hummingbird story. They are upmarket from Lola's, I would say (though their cupcakes are around the same price, just north of £3 for a red velvet in both cases), and they opened a little earlier, in 2004.

Their flagship branch is in what might be described as an American's idea of a trendy London street, Portobello Road, internationally famous for its antique market, and in what might be described as an American's idea of a trendy London area, Notting Hill, which was already well on the way to prohibitive property prices before it was immortalised in the schlocky film of the same name.

There is often a considerable queue outside that branch for takeaway cupcakes, but the Victoria set-up is less photogenic and I was in and out in a flash. Actually Victoria is Hummingbird's only branch in a less-than-fashionable area (the others being in Spitalfields, St John's Wood and South Kensington), and it is less than surprising to learn that they have a franchise operation in Dubai, which really ought to have a London postcode of its own.

Finished! And I remembered at once my personal rule that one red velvet cupcake is enough, even if that cupcake is as tempting as Hummingbird's red velvet. It is simply too rich for repetition.

I needed a breath of fresh air after two cupcakes in a row, and decided that I could finish off the cupcake chapterette, the cupcake interlude, after a short walk that would take me, with a hint of renewed appetite, to the ideal spot to conclude the chapter: Peggy Porschen's shop, the throne room of Belgravia's queen of cupcakes.

It struck me, as I walked north from Victoria into Belgravia, the land of silk and money, that this had been a Londoncentric experience. I'm sorry about that, but I think it's fair to say that a cupcake is much the same no matter where you consume it, and that the finest cupcake emporium of any sizeable town is unlikely to be markedly different in concept or execution from Hummingbird or Lola's.

The same is true of the cupcakes at Peggy Porschen, but this is a business that accepts the fact that presentation is a substantial part of any cupcake's appeal, and ensures that its production values are more Beverly Hills than *Great British Bake Off*.

Peggy herself is a former airline flight attendant, and one has to assume that she worked primarily in First Class. She makes cupcakes for people who only know how to turn left upon boarding; cupcakes for A-listers... or at least people who want a taste of the First Class A-lister life, for the price of a (startlingly expensive) cupcake.

Her shop is at the southern end of Elizabeth Street, the last gasp of swanky Belgravia before it becomes unspeakable Victoria. It is a remarkable emporium, pastel pink with pink and white awnings and vast pink and white 'ribbon' bows. There is an arch of convincing but fake flowers over the door-way, and swags of the same flowers along the window-sills.

The approach to the doorway is guarded by queue ropes strung between gold pillars, like those protecting the red carpet at a movie premiere except that here, of course, even the ropes are pink.

The gap in the ropes is guarded by an emphatic, printed (pink lettering), framed notice: 'PLEASE WAIT here to be seated or take away'.

CUPCAKES

I did what I was told (I'm British: if I'm told to form a queue, I comply, even if I am the only one in it, and there is clearly no need for it). But not for long. It was cold, and starting to rain, and there was no one ahead of me in the queue, or in the shop. The idea was to give the impression of clamouring crowds even when there were none, and it should be pointed out in Peggy's defence that in summer there often is a queue, though people seem as keen to be photographed under the floral arch as they are to buy anything.

I pushed open the door, and no one objected. The ceiling was strung with fairy lights; a framed watercolour of the floral arch hung on the wall with the slogan: 'A world where cake becomes a living art and roses always bloom'. A world where the cupcakes cost £7 each and the roses always bloom because they're fake.

Two of the half dozen tiny tables were occupied, each by a pair of smartly dressed young customers; at each table a selfie was being taken as I placed my order.

I asked for a red velvet – see how quickly my resolve wore off? – and a Black Forest and sat at a table in the corner, next to a display of branded birthday candles.

I attacked the red velvet first, and immediately regretted my choice; the sponge was tough and claggy, and tasted of nothing at all; the frosting was generously swirled and sprinkled with sugar hearts to pretty effect, but tasted of sugar and little else.

This is an item whose primary purpose is visual: it is the fate of many a cupcake to be consumed as photo-fodder rather than food. They are made with selfies in mind, and Peggy

Porschen's are Instagram-primed: attractive and immaculate in appearance, ready for their close-up.

The Belgravia boutique opened in 2010, and there is another in Chelsea; Peggy's husband Bryn, a former chef with kitchen superstars Marcus Wareing and Angela Hartnett, is managing director, while Peggy gets the creative credit.

It's hard to fault her eye, at least, but I wasn't about to fall in love with the taste of her red velvet. I set it aside, ruined but not finished. I had higher hopes of the Black Forest version, and remembered a tip from my elder daughter, to whom I had been whingeing about the impossibility of eating these things without getting them up my nose.

'There's a trick to it, don't you know?' Lucy had said, with a God-Dad-get-with-the-century eye-roll. She had demonstrated with a stray Hummingbird vanilla cupcake at home, neatly tearing off the bottom half of the sponge and swiftly plonking it down on top of the frosting, to make an instant sandwich cake that was suddenly a much more civilised prospect for public consumption.

'Where did you learn that?' I asked, lost in admiration.

'Can't remember. Someone showed me. TikTok, probably.'

I tried the TikTok hack with my Black Forest cupcake and just about succeeded, landing only one blob of frosting on my sweater, which my fellow customers were too self-obsessed to notice.

It was much nicer than PP's red velvet: luscious sponge, well-textured frosting and a delicious as well as decorative black cherry on top that brought a most welcome hit of genuine flavour to the party.

I polished it off in three bites with pleasure: under different circumstances – say, had I not previously consumed three other cupcakes – I might have ordered another. But I felt slightly sick, and slightly ashamed.

That's enough about cupcakes, don't you think? It's not really a chapter, but then they're not really cakes. Shall we just call it an interlude – a slightly embarrassing interlude? Let's do that, and move on.

THE HUMMINGBIRD BAKERY'S RED VELVET CUPCAKES

There's only room for one cupcake recipe, and it really had to be the classic American cupcake that has had the biggest impact on British culinary life.

To make a red velvet layer cake instead, double the quantities below, divide between three 20cm cake tins, and bake for 25 minutes at the same oven temperature.

TIP: For the classic decoration, trim a little off the top of each cooled cupcake before icing, and crumble finely into a bowl. After you've frosted the cakes, scatter with these red velvet crumbs.

CAKE

120g soft unsalted butter

300g caster sugar

2 large eggs

20g cocoa powder

1 tbsp red food-colouring paste, such as
Sugarflair in Red Extra

1 tsp vanilla extract

240ml buttermilk

300g plain flour

1 tsp fine sea salt

1 tsp bicarbonate of soda

3 tsp white vinegar

Cream cheese frosting

100g soft unsalted butter

600g icing sugar

250g full-fat cream cheese, chilled

1. Preheat the oven to 180°C/350F/Gas Mark 4. Put 16 paper baking cases into the holes of a cupcake tin or tins.
2. Put the butter and sugar into an electric stand mixer with a paddle attachment (or use an electric hand mixer) and beat on medium speed until light and fluffy and well mixed.
3. Turn the mixer up to high speed, slowly add the eggs and beat until well incorporated.
4. In a separate bowl, mix together the cocoa powder, red food-colouring and vanilla extract to make a

thick, dark paste. Add to the butter mixture and mix thoroughly until evenly combined and coloured (scrape any unmixed ingredients from the inside of the bowl with a rubber spatula).

5. Turn the mixer down to slow speed and slowly pour in half the buttermilk. Beat until well mixed, then add half the flour and beat until well incorporated. Repeat this process until all the buttermilk and flour have been added. Scrape down the side of the bowl again. Turn the mixer up to high speed and beat until smooth and even. Turn the mixer down to low speed and add the salt, bicarb and vinegar. Beat until well mixed, then turn up the speed again and beat for a couple more minutes.

6. Spoon the batter into the paper baking cups until one-third full. Bake in the oven for 20–25 minutes, or until the cupcakes bounce back when touched. A skewer inserted in the centre should come out clean. Let the cupcakes cool for about 15 minutes in the tin before inverting them on to a wire rack to cool completely.

7. While the cupcakes are cooling, make the frosting. Beat the butter and icing sugar together in a free-standing mixer with a paddle attachment (or use an electric hand mixer) on a medium-slow speed until the mixture comes together and is well mixed – cover with a tea towel to stop the icing sugar going everywhere. It will have a sandy texture. Add the cream cheese all in one go and beat until fully

incorporated. Turn the mixer up to a medium-high speed. Continue beating until the frosting is light and fluffy – at least 5 minutes – but do not overbeat, as it can quickly become runny.

8. When the cupcakes are cold, spoon the cream cheese frosting on to each cupcake, gently smoothing it over with a metal spatula and creating a swirl of frosting on each one. Remember the tip above about sprinkling the tops with crumbs.

CHAPTER 10
BIRTHDAY CAKES — AND COLIN

The invasion of Britain by cupcakes, and the resulting eclipse of the native fairy cake, brings the story of cakes in British life closer to our present times. But in order to consider a cake that plays an important role in all of our lives at least once a year, we first need to rewind a little... more than a little. Half a century or so.

The earliest birthday that I can remember is not one of mine. It was an early birthday – perhaps his fifth – of my friend Mark, who recently came to a birthday party of mine more than five decades later.

Unlike me, with just the one younger brother, Mark had three older siblings, so his parents had plenty of practice at hosting birthday parties. For this one, they decided on fancy dress, which meant that Mark got to dress up as a cowboy with, I remember with great clarity and a little residual bitterness, fringed trousers and a stonking Colt 45 cap gun.

My mother decided that my brother and I should both go as Baker Boys, and fashioned us chef's toques out of white plastic bags with card headbands, on which – in case anyone had missed the point, the words 'Baker Boy' were written in black felt-tip. We were each equipped, I clearly recall, with a wooden spoon from the kitchen drawer: had Instagram been invented in 1967, we'd have been all over it.

What I don't remember anything about – from this party or any of the many other birthday parties that I attended throughout my youth – is the cake.

In those days, the cake wasn't such a big deal at a birthday party. It was there, and great effort had no doubt gone into it, since it would have to have been made, almost certainly by the hosting mother or a close relative of hers. It would not have been anything as fancy as a Battenberg cake. A plain sponge along Victoria lines, with jam in the middle, a thin layer of icing on top, like thawing snow, and candles. That was it.

A little later on, at parties for slightly older children with less propensity for throwing up, cakes became chocolate and more substantial.

But they still weren't works of art, startling replicas of vehicles or sporting implements or film stars. They weren't sold in supermarkets, either: nor did they inspire lengthy and expensive court cases. That would all follow in the next century.

Round about the time that I was growing out of cake (temporarily) and starting to focus my birthday celebrations on alcohol, British birthday cakes – and celebration cakes in general – were given a great creative boost by the widely publicised creations of the already famous Jane Asher, who, in the early 1980s, became known for her witty and artistic cakes.

Asher was first in the public eye as a child actress in the 1950s. In the Sixties she swung with the best of them, appeared in a lot of movies (not all of them good), and was a major influence on the style of the Beatles as Paul McCartney's beautiful, red-haired long-term girlfriend. By the end of the Seventies, she was married to the cartoonist Gerald Scarfe (as she still is to this day), bringing up young children and winning great esteem among London's beau monde for her fabulous celebration cakes.

Asher's book *Party Cakes* was published as a lavish, full-colour, large-format book in 1982 and had a huge impact on the baking scene at that time. The author had long moved in the circles of accomplished creative people, and the book has something of the style of the best Sunday newspaper colour supplements of the time: the cakes look great, and are beautifully photographed with beautiful people who are related to each recipe (and some of the children featured are now famous grown-ups, which adds to the charm).

I mention the book not so much because the recipes were especially innovative or the baking unusual or challenging, but because of the impact it had on the wider baking public, decades before the advent of *The Great British Bake Off* convinced us all that creative baking could be fun and that startling results were achievable at home.

Asher's book not only did wonders for awareness of creative baking, it also did wonders for the sugar industry, because – with all due respect – most of her creations were ordinary cakes rendered extraordinary by the lavish and creative use of colossal quantities of Plasticine-like fondant icing.

With Asher's book propped up in front of them and a bulk order of fondant and food colouring, parents and other party preparers could look beyond an iced sponge or chocolate sponge roll to a slab of lurid green football pitch surmounted by stumpy sporting figurines in their child's chosen colours, or a fairly convincing, if bulky, ballerina or pop star.

These days there are websites devoted solely to cake decoration from which one can order edible 'toppers' related to the most obscure hobbies and pastimes.

Those doing the catering can, if they wish, bake a basic cake to go under the acreage of bought-in adornments, or they can buy a chunk of sponge or ginger or whatever and simply do an assembly job.

In either case they can – with differing levels of justification – claim 'I made it myself' as the guests tuck in. A certain amount of pride is at stake here, and given that every party is to some extent an exercise in showing off on the part of the hosts, a home-made cake is an obvious vehicle for ostentatious display.

The modern form of birthday cake – as we would recognise it, with candles denoting the recipient's age, and so on – is first reliably reported from what is now Germany but was then a bunch of smaller kingdoms and dukedoms, in the eighteenth century. How reliably reported? One of the earliest mentions is in the journal of the playwright and poet Goethe, who attended a prince's birthday party, with candle-laden cake, in 1801. I will certainly take his word for it.

Less reliable accounts suggest that in earlier times Bavarian children would be given a cake on the morning of their birthday, with a lit candle in it, and the candle would be replaced as it burnt down by another, and so on until the early evening, when the child was finally allowed a slice of their cake, which by now was presumably almost invisible under a layer of wax.

I'm not sure what the reasoning was behind such a lengthy exercise in delayed gratification, but it seems not so much a matter for Goethe as for Jung or even Freud.

Perhaps, though, the early Germans were simply anticipating modern practice, in which the candle or candles have become as important as the cake, the edible element merely a vehicle for the symbolic flame.

In my time I have helped provide some splendid vehicles, though. I can remember my daughters' early birthday parties. Sort of. They are in their mid-twenties now, so their first post-infancy bashes were two decades ago, and the memories kind of blend together into an amalgam of games, smiles, tears and wrapping paper. I think I spent most of my time filming with an actual video camera – this was before smartphones – because what any parent wants most from a birthday is not only that their child should enjoy themself, but that there should be a permanent and comprehensive record of this occurring.

So I'm a bit sketchy on the detail, but having consulted my daughters I can confirm that the most memorable elements of these parties were a skunk called Lily and two cakes.

Lily was an all-white skunk who was the star turn of a man who, for a considerable fee, would bring a van full of animals to your child's party and pass them around. He had a chinchilla and a tarantula, but Lily was the one that all the little girls wanted to cuddle. 'She's been de-stinked,' my elder daughter, Lucy, told me as she stroked the animal's head.

The cake, at that same party, was another white animal: a remarkable rendition of Hedwig, the boy wizard's owl from the Harry Potter franchise.

Hedwig – or rather an accurate two-dimensional portrait of the bird – had been crafted out of flat layers of white and grey fondant icing on a jam sponge base by the mother of one of my daughters' friends, who had once foolishly admitted to making the impressive cake for her own child's party and had since been besieged by other parents with their own commissions.

My younger daughter, Emily, also remembers a remarkable cake from one of her parties – not so much the cake, to be precise, as the decoration: a sugarwork sculpture of her favourite soft toy, a battered grey-striped cat called KitCat. This was not the work of another mother but of a specialist who worked from photographs of pets or toys to produce startlingly accurate representations in solid icing sugar which could then sit – as KitCat had – on top of a regular cake, to the universal admiration of the partygoers, who knew how devoted my daughter was to her toy.

The sculpture was so good – so like the real thing – that Emily expressly forbade his consumption. He was conveyed carefully away from the party resting on napkins in a Tupperware box... in which he remained, on a high shelf in the kitchen, for many years. I wouldn't be at all surprised to find that SugarCat is still among my daughter's most treasured possessions, along with the soft toy that inspired him, and who is still very much a presence in Emily's life.

I'm not at all sure that animal parties are still a popular presence in small children's social lives. I suspect that a de-stinked skunk would draw concerned questions from other parents, if not from welfare-alert children: 'Daddy, exactly how do you de-stink a skunk? And isn't that chinchilla overheating?'

Birthdays at my age are still fun, of course, but perhaps a little less imaginative. For my most recent birthday dinner, for example, I was presented – at the end of a fine meal with friends and family – with a single lit candle inserted into a slab of baklava. Not strictly a cake, but the candle made it occasion-appropriate.

Earlier that day, courtesy of my kindly colleagues, I had enjoyed another kind of birthday cake. Not German, or Greek, or lavishly and inventively home-made. For my co-workers are wise and practical people, and they know that for a no-fuss informal party, just as for a no-holds-barred children's bash, there is no need for a cake at all, when you can opt for a caterpillar instead.

This is where the chapter takes a swerve. Because in admitting that a birthday cake can take almost any form that is relevant to the star guest, I admit that I can't track down a True Slice. Mine was baklava. Yours might be cheesecake. Or cheese, come to that. But there cannot be any doubt that ever since his invention, Colin the Caterpillar has been at more British birthday parties than any other invertebrate you can mention.

Indeed, in the annals of British cake history there has never been a phenomenon to match Colin.

He's just a chocolate sponge roll with a chocolate butter-cream filling – the kind of thing, in fact, that an accomplished home baker might have served up for a birthday party in the 1960s.

But since his launch by Marks & Spencer almost thirty-three years ago, Colin has become the UK's unquestioned cake champion. More than 15 million Colin the Caterpillar cakes have been sold in the UK, a number still increasing by half a million a year, and Colin has fathered (if that is what caterpillars do) a brand family of Marks & Spencer's items that bear his gormless features – or in the case of the packets of Colin faces, consist of nothing but his gormless features – as well as numerous other very similar items produced by rival retailers.

Colin's face has developed quite a bit since his original iteration, in 1990, when he was a very rudimentary item indeed: just a chocolate Swiss roll with a milk chocolate shell, a sprinkling of Smartie-sized sugar spots and a flat white chocolate disc for a face with a cross-eyed expression printed on it.

Some have suggested that Colin was inspired by a caterpillar creation in Jane Asher's book. But I have a copy of that book, and while there is a lovely snail there is no caterpillar.

Others claim that the inspiration was Eric Carle's wonderful children's book *The Very Hungry Caterpillar*, and it would be a nice irony if something that is designed to be eaten had indeed been inspired by something that loves to eat.

But that book was first published at least twenty years before Colin's conception, and Marks & Spencer's current cake experts say they have no evidence that Carle's creature inspired theirs.

The official version – and I had a team from M&S kindly check this out for me – is that Colin arose through the joint efforts of Marks & Spencer's product designers and developers at Park Cakes, the company who have made cakes for M&S for more than eighty years, and who still make the Colin cakes today.

In the 1980s the M&S party cake range was all about round cakes topped with a slab of icing bearing a two-dimensional character face. The collaborators, getting down to work in 1989, wanted to come up with something that was 'different, that could be easily portioned and would have wide appeal to customers.'

Many trials were undertaken of character cakes in bar shapes, before they finally hit on a chocolate sponge roll as the best basis. A number of different characters were tested, but one emerged triumphant: Colin the Caterpillar was born!

According to my expert sources at M&S HQ, Colin 'hit the ground running' despite his lack of actual legs, and quickly became a bestseller in their stores. I don't know about you, but I feel there might be a West End musical in this one day.

How he has evolved! These days Colin has a much chunkier, 3D-sculpted white chocolate face, a set of white chocolate feet and a range of costume makeovers dependent on time of year and occasion. He also has a spouse, Connie, who shares the same basic components but is filled with strawberry butter-cream and has berry-flavoured feet.

Giant versions of Colin and Connie – the stuff of nightmares, frankly, if they were real caterpillars – serve forty people, and there are variations on the standard models for Halloween (Count Colin, given a vampiric makeover and added sugary creepy-crawlies), Easter (Colin grows bunny ears) and Christmas (he wears a Santa hat and is accessorised with candy canes and the like).

Once M&S realised that Colin's face was a valuable perk for the party-giver, and that it could be the subject of altercations among grown-up party guests, they launched packets containing nothing but Colin faces, a deeply weird notion if you give it any thought, but very useful for pacifying fractious children (and their parents).

The brand was extended to cupcakes, jelly sweets, cookie dough biscuits and Colin in a Jar, the marmalised invertebrate in food-on-the-go form.

Long before these iterations hit the shelves, Colin had broken out of the children's party market to become a staple of the office bash, perhaps because by now he has a certain kitsch retro appeal among people who remember him from their childhood birthday parties but are now fully grown marketing executives, senior nurses and national newspaper journalists, but also, I suspect, because he remains sugary, unchallenging and easy to cut and share out – until you get to the face, of course.

All of this success has, inevitably, inspired other retailers to come up with rival caterpillars, in one case provoking a lengthy and expensive legal case.

Perhaps you have come across one or more of Colin's rivals. Perhaps you prefer them to the original. In an ever more standardised world, where supermarkets compete more often on price than originality, the name and quirks of each chain's caterpillar cake are a rare point of difference. For all I know there are spotters combing the country noting minor updates in facial expression or limb count among this weird clan, or academic researchers in the field of marketing plotting every development.

CRUMBS OF KNOWLEDGE
COLIN V. CUTHBERT: THE SUPERMARKET CATERPILLAR CAKE WARS

The names alone of the supermarket caterpillar cohort speak volumes: Colin and Connie we have met, and I must admit that they are the baked invertebrates with which I am most familiar. Up against them are ranged Cuthbert, of Aldi, of whom more below; Clyde from Asda; Cecil from Waitrose; Charlie from the Co-Op; Curly from Tesco, Clive from OneStop and — bravely departing from the C Section, Wiggles from Sainsbury's. Free-from variants include Frieda from Asda (see what they did there?); Carl from Tesco and Eric from Sainsburys, the latter two perhaps nodding to the author of *The Very Hungry Caterpillar*, Eric Carle.

Most recently, to coincide with the Coronation of King Charles III, Waitrose brought out Jewel the Jack Russell, who is disguised with a crown and a face not entirely unlike that of the monarch, and claims to be a small dog, but still looks very much like a caterpillar to me.

Of all these, Cuthbert has attracted the most attention, not through originality or outstanding culinary achievement, but through the courts. In April 2021, newspapers were delighted to note Marks & Spencer's announcement that it had lodged an intellectual property claim for infringement of three trademarks with the High Court against Aldi in relation to their rival's Cuthbert the Caterpillar. In its complaint, Marks & Spencer claimed that Aldi's Cuthbert the Caterpillar was too similar to their own Colin the Caterpillar cake, which could lead consumers to believe that they were of the same standard and would allow Cuthbert to 'ride on the coat-tails' of the M&S cake's reputation. I'm not sure that caterpillars – or indeed cakes – have coat-tails, but that is of no importance because in February 2022, the lawsuit was settled between both parties for an undisclosed amount.

One of the key missions I have assigned to myself in each of the chapters of this book is the pursuit of the True Slice: a version of each of the cakes under consideration that is authentic or ideal or splendid or at the very least deeply appropriate, to be consumed in a location that is relevant to the cake concerned.

In the case of Colin the Caterpillar the question of authenticity has been debated and decided at a most elevated legal level. It is not for me to quibble with the judgements of the bench. I simply had to secure a genuine Marks & Spencer Colin, not one of his relatives and certainly not one of the rival caterpillars sold by other retailers. Not difficult. King Arthur would hardly have considered it a quest worth getting out of bed for.

The question of where to consume the Colin might have been solved equally easily. I am blessed with a multitude of small relations or quasi-relations, and their birthdays crop up on a regular basis. Hardly a month seems to go by without the need to secure some kind of age-appropriate, environmentally friendly and educationally enhancing item for presentation to the deserving child, and while attendance at their birthday parties is not compulsory I am certainly welcome, and fully entitled to my slice of Colin (though almost certainly not to his face).

But while appropriate, this didn't seem quite enough. Perhaps, I felt, it lacked the element of challenge required to maintain the pulse-racing, page-turning excitement that the modern cake-book reader demands.

Further thought required. The reason I decided to focus on Colin in this chapter is not just because he exemplifies the modern birthday cake. As a hard-working, widely available cake he is often employed for other purposes, after all. He also earned inclusion on his unique status as a cake brand – a deliberately invented product that has earned millions for his creators and inspired a family of related cakes and treats, not to mention an army of similar rival entities.

So perhaps the right place to eat a True Slice of Colin is as close as possible to the nerve centre of the organisation that created him. Now, where does Marks & Spencer live?

The long-established company's long-established HQ was on Baker Street in London, just a few hundred yards south of the home of another venerable and respected British institution, Sherlock Holmes. But just a couple of years ago M&S moved to a home away from Holmes, about half a mile to the west on the banks of a little regarded, but these days rather smart, London waterway.

There is a watery junction in central London where the Grand Union Canal, having travelled from Birmingham, becomes the Regent's Canal for the last few miles of its journey to the Thames; the lake, or pond, where the two canals meet is known as Browning's Pool and sits at the heart of the once louche and now fashionable district of Little Venice. But there is another, abortive offshoot from Browning's Pool, which passes under multiple road bridges (one of them carrying the vast Westway) and runs for half a mile past Paddington Station and St Mary's Hospital to terminate rather pointlessly in a dead end up against the insalubrious Edgware Road.

For decades this area was very derelict indeed, one of the last remaining undeveloped sites in the middle of the capital. But over the last ten years it has suddenly sprouted office blocks and luxury flats, hemmed in on all sides by busy roads, railways and the old canal.

Into this shiny but strange area Marks and Spencer parachuted their HQ.

In the basement of their offices is a very shiny branch of the store, one in which I imagine the staff are pretty much permanently on best behaviour. When I visited one morning I found a handful of picnic tables outside the store, and a variety of Colins on sale inside. I was tempted to score a full-sized Colin, nab a little wooden knife from the office food section and saw away at him at one of the outdoor tables.

But when I had looked up the location of the HQ I'd noticed an M&S café in the same block, and that seemed to me to offer an even more authentic location.

So I cut along the canal bank for another fifty metres, then went through a very slow revolving door and into the ground floor of a vast, pristine office building.

The M&S café was a modest affair with windows overlooking the dead end of the canal and a hospital car park. Two middle-aged ladies were serving behind the counter.

'I'd like some Colin the Caterpillar cake, please,' I announced.

'Sorry dear,' one lady replied. 'We don't have any. The cakes we've got are all there...' she pointed at a table behind me: triple layer carrot cake; salted caramel tiffin squares. Clearly no Colin.

I must have looked very disappointed.

'If it's Colin you're after, there's always... that,' the second lady suggested. She indicated the 'Iced Drinks' board behind her on the wall.

Colin the Caterpillar Frappé.

A few noisy moments (and £3.75) later I sat a table next to the window, regarding Colin's sweet, trusting, white-chocolate face as it grinned up at me from a transparent plastic beaker in the grey winter light.

His disembodied features, smiling bravely, sat atop a glistening pile of chocolatey foam. It was like the denouement of a Hammer Horror movie, and the more I thought about it the more monstrous it seemed, with overtones of *Frankenstein* or *Theatre of Blood*. This sweet, trusting creature, who had brought so much pleasure to so many, had been taken by his own people, by his family – even, to push it to the extreme – his parents... and put in a blender. Frappéd.

But duty called. It was hardly a slice, but in a sense this was the apotheosis of Colin, the cake that became a brand, spawning offspring of every kind conceivable, and some inconceivable.

I took a cautious slurp. Actually, it didn't taste all that bad – which shouldn't be surprising, because M&S don't, to my knowledge, sell anything that tastes actively disgusting. It was essentially a chocolate milkshake, with overtones of sugary cakiness, and the texture, thank goodness, was smooth rather than lumpy. I slurped, considered, slurped again... and became aware of my fellow customers in the café, none of whom were consuming Colin Frappés, and several of whom were looking at me with expressions that varied from curiosity to frank disgust.

I could understand why. For one thing, it was breakfast time. For another, the Colin Frappé may have tasted acceptable, to a seasoned and shameless cake consumer, but it looked ghastly: a tall glass of brown liquid, topped with a pile of thick brown goo and surmounted with a little face. It was... horrid.

Forgive me for not providing a recipe for a make-your-own Colin. Marks & Spencer would much rather you went and bought one, and I don't wish to annoy their lawyers.

CHAPTER 11
CHOCOLATE CAKE

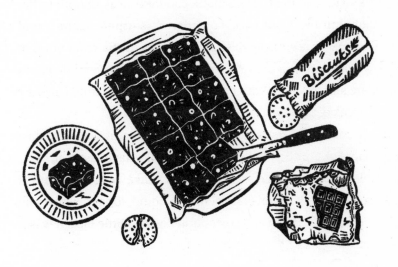

After all the attention we have just paid to Colin the Caterpillar, it will be apparent to many of you that he could entirely justifiably take up a lot of space in this chapter too. He is, unquestionably, a chocolate cake, and a good example of the way in which a simple concept has expanded to embrace an amazingly varied range of possibilities.

The appeal is obvious: chocolate is lovely, cake is lovely, so combining the two ought to mean loveliness squared. Most of the time, it works: 'chocolate cake' figures in the top three of every survey I have ever seen of Britons' favourite form of cake. Chocolate fudge cake – just saying the name makes me drool – is a staple on mass-market restaurant menus, and the chocolate fondant is a recurring symbol of triumph and disaster in every series of *MasterChef*.

It's just generic: 'chocolate cake' means pretty much any cake that involves chocolate, and very often people who like their cakes to involve chocolate are not all that fussy about what form this involvement takes. This ambiguity makes my quest to find a True Slice perhaps more challenging than it was for the Eccles from Eccles: in this chapter I'm not looking for a perfect example of a specific kind of cake from a specific place, more the perfect combination of chocolate, and cake, and an idea of Britishness.

First of all, let's go back down the Proustian path to my childhood memories of chocolate cake, which seem to centre mainly on mini-rolls.

In fact I was born in the same year as the mini-roll, which came into being, like me, in 1962. They are essentially, of course, mini Swiss rolls – a term first recorded in this country in a Birmingham Baker's advertisement from the 1850s. Cadbury's still make their miniature version in Liverpool, in the same factory complex that has produced them since the year of my birth.

I remember them as an after-tea treat at the better kind of friend's household when I was a child: the kind of friend who may well have had a miniature football goal at one end of their garden, or a Raleigh Chopper that they were prepared to let me ride, or an older brother with a drum kit or an electric guitar.

Their mother would serve cheese sandwiches (white bread only) in which the cheese was actually Cheddar and sliced rather than grated. There might even have been actual Coca-Cola rather than the insipid imitation from a Sodastream. Then there would be a plate of mini-rolls which, in my mind's eye, were wrapped in silver and purple shrouds of thin foil – I can hear the faint crinkle of it being unwrapped now.

And I can remember the physical sensation more accurately than the taste: biting through the thin shell of milk chocolate to the soft sponge within, and the slushy sweet filling within that. Each little bar supplied three bites for me: two for a hungrier friend.

To help jog my memory – such arduous research I have had to undertake for this project, your heart must bleed – I bought a box of this year's model.

They were redesigned (of course! I am the only thing I know from 1962 that hasn't been redesigned), by a consultancy called Robot Food, in 2015. I looked up some of the background material on this project, and it seems that Cadbury's were concerned that their mini-rolls were too easily confused with supermarket own-brand mini-rolls, with very good reason.

Robot decided that the little swirl of goo in the middle of a mini-roll should become the key selling point, so they made it look like a quote mark, and covered the wrappers in what must have seemed at the time like smart, sassy quotes.

Or, as Robot put it: 'We capitalised on the speech mark shape created by the swirled filling and developed a positioning "with BIG personality". The new brand lock-up is bold and fun, and we heroed each product with dynamic photography. These were brought to life with a series of relevant exclamations to give each flavour literal shelf shout.'

I shudder to think how much people get paid to come up with this guff. Inside the witty wrappers it's still a little chocolate cylinder, and the ingredients are still a parent's nightmare of sugar, palm oil and E-numbers. I tried one. I tried two, actually, just be sure, but the spell was broken, the magical childhood appeal vanished forever... for me, at least.

CAKE

These little sugary torpedoes have been part of British life for more than half a century now, and notwithstanding the rebrand they still exert a nostalgic pull. But despite Cadbury's efforts to big up their heritage – they have a museum/theme park at their Bourneville factory, which I have visited, and don't recommend – I don't feel that the mini-roll justifies a quest for a True Slice.

The same goes, I'm afraid, for chocolate fudge cake, which may be many people's idea of a perfect combination of chocolate and cake. Don't get me wrong: I can see the appeal, and have in my time put away many a soft, dark, sugary slab... but I don't feel any kind of cultural connection with it, and I couldn't find a compelling back-story of any kind. Delicious, undoubtedly: interesting, less so.

I wondered if the title of True Slice might be accorded instead to another kind of chocolate cake altogether, one that has decades of fame, and a certain amount of notoriety, at the other end of the social scale from the Tesco baked goods aisle: the River Café's Chocolate Nemesis.

It sounds like a dubious Batman villain from the days before the franchise started to take itself too seriously, but Chocolate Nemesis has some claims to being the most celebrated – in some ways the most notorious – British chocolate cake of this century. If, that is, that you accept that it is a cake at all.

On the 'Looks like a duck, quacks like a duck' principle, I contend that Nemesis, ever-present on the menu at the River Café in Hammersmith in West London for the last twenty-five years, is a cake. It arrives on a plate, looking like a slab of chocolate cake. When the diner tucks in (with a spoon), it cuts – and tastes – like a cake, albeit one conceived and executed by the culinary gods. It's a cake.

A flourless cake, I'm going to call it, drawing a veil over other descriptions that I have seen, such as 'firm custard' and 'egg dessert', which are neither evocative nor appealing. 'Mousse cake' is another name it has been called, and I'll accept that: it's a mousse that can be cut and served in slices, a mousse with what one might call a crust, if that didn't conjure unpleasant visions. Perhaps it is best to stick to the name its creators gave it: Nemesis. Deep, dark and deadly delicious – and often spelling doom, or at least serious embarrassment, for those who attempt to make it at home.

The River Café was founded in 1987 by Rose Gray and Ruth Rogers, growing out of the canteen for staff at the architectural firm of Rogers's husband Richard. That's why it's located in an unusual spot (for a restaurant): the ground floor of an office building – a stylishly designed office building, but still an office building – down by the river on a distant back-street in unfashionable Hammersmith.

The friends' spin on Italian cooking quickly attracted a knowledgeable and influential crowd, and soon they were all talking about, and attempting to emulate at home, the restaurant's marvellous chocolate cake, named Nemesis and adapted from a recipe that Gray and Rogers had seen in a magazine in 1988. It first appeared on the restaurant menu in 1989, and has been there ever since.

It was a byword for difficulty, said to be all but impossible for home cooks to replicate, even after the recipe was published in the first of many River Café cookbooks.

In his book *The Pedant in the Kitchen* the novelist Julian Barnes, a keen amateur cook, recounts a scene from an early 1990s dinner party:

> *On a sideboard is a plate on which squats something circular, brown and sloshy, and definitely not looking its best – a kind of cowpat, really.*
>
> *Sympathetic guest: Chocolate Nemesis?*
> *Hostess: Yes.*
> *Sympathetic guest: Didn't work.*
> *Hostess: No.*
> *Sympathetic guest: Never does.*
> *Hostess: I've made some other puddings instead.*

Anyone with any pretensions to competence in the kitchen at this time – a particularly intense culinary era, when London was emerging as a force on the international food scene, chefs such as Gordon Ramsay and Marco Pierre White were in their pomp and the term 'foodie' was first widely used – attempted to make Chocolate Nemesis at home, and not all were as brave as Barnes's hostess in publicly displaying their failures on the sideboard. Goodness knows how many near-miss Nemesisses were simply sloshed into the bin.

I've never tried to cook it: way above my competence levels. But I have eaten it, a dozen or so times in as many years, and always where it should be eaten: at the River Café itself.

I'm very fortunate in having friends and relatives prepared to treat me to a meal in this remarkable – and remarkably expensive – restaurant once a year. I almost always have the chilli squid to start with, hot scarlet flecks on seared cephalopod, usually a simple, fresh pasta dish to follow that, nothing too substantial, because always, without fail, the Chocolate Nemesis to finish.

The appeal for me, as a fan of proper chocolate, is that the quality of this most important ingredient is showcased by the cake. The restaurant doesn't mention any particular brand, and nor did Gray and Rogers in the recipe's earliest days, but the River Café is all about Italian food and carefully sourced ingredients. River Café recipe books stipulate 'best quality 70% cocoa solids chocolate' and top quality Italian chocolate has a style all of its own, shiny and crisp: if I had to guess, I'd go for one of the 70% bars made by the Domori company on the outskirts of Turin.

I digress. Whenever I am about to enjoy a slice of this cake, nothing distracts me: not the conversation of my friends, the banter of the waiting staff, the chatter of the fashionable crowd. These are a few moments of intense pleasure, powerful flavour and delicate texture combining to exquisite effect.

It's a measure of the dish's balance, I think, that it doesn't seem to induce gluttony in the way that an inferior chocolate cake might: one slice is always enough. Then I can sit back and digest, and take in the scene, enjoy the bustle, the chefs at work in full view, the evening's complement of movers, shakers and celebrities at other tables.

So that is a True Slice accounted for, and in its appropriate location. But still it doesn't seem to tick all the right boxes.

Perhaps it is the comparative youth of the cake, or its clearly Italian provenance (it is related to any number of regional Italian recipes, flourless for religious festival reasons and varying according to local practice). Perhaps it is simply too much of a plutocrats' plaything, at £14 a slice and usually terminating a £100 meal... in any case I don't think it is worthy of the culmination of a quest. If you disagree, you can order it online for home delivery: £35 for the cake, but you have to source your own celebrities.

My next chocolate cake is much easier to make. That is, it is much easier to make adequately. But a really good brownie is hard to find. Some say the brownie, like the cupcake, is irretrievably American. But I say that this is one of those cakes that the British have taken to their hearts – possibly at some risk to their circulation. Like chocolate fudge cake they are eaten with gusto up and down the UK, which, to my mind, makes them at the very least worthy of exploration. And unlike chocolate fudge cake, there is an interesting back-story and at least one uniquely interesting British maker.

I remember being amazed by the proficiency of friends who produced brilliant brownies in student kitchens; it remains a much more achievable creation for the amateur chef than the Chocolate Nemesis or the fickle fondant. But a really good brownie is still worth a long journey.

To Sheffield, for instance, which may not immediately strike one as the likeliest location of a delectable chocolate brownie, but that it most certainly is.

The train to south Yorkshire from London takes almost exactly two hours, most of which I spent trying to make sense of the variety of claimants to the title of Inventor of the Chocolate Brownie, and falling down a series of Googleholes in the process.

Brownie heritage is certainly a complex area, and one about which online commentators can become quite heated. One muddling issue is that the term 'brownie' applies not only to baked goods but also to a variety of elf. Big Ears, for example, the well-known companion of Noddy, is a brownie, and the junior branch of the Girl Guides was named after these mischievous creatures.

These sorts of brownies seem to have a Scottish or Celtic origin, and they feature in the title of a novel by the Scottish writer James Hogg published in 1818. Children's writers in the US prompted a widespread brownie mania in the late nineteenth century, which was just about the time that cooks were starting to come up with delicious baked, but not risen, squares, also called brownies.

Many well-meaning but easily confused commentators have conflated these two (it seems to me) separate trends, thus muddling the origin of the baked brownie up with the popularity of the pixies. Guys, it's just a coincidence.

The little baked squares – which may first have been flavoured with molasses rather than chocolate – are called brownies because they are brown. Nothing whatsoever to do with Big Ears and his pals.

On the basis of the evidence that I reviewed on the train to Sheffield, I am persuaded that the chocolate brownie was invented in or around 1893 by a chef called Joseph Stehl, who worked at the Palmer House Hotel in Chicago. The proprietor of the Palmer House, Bertha Palmer, was a leading figure in city society and wanted to ensure that visitors to the World's Columbian Exposition, held there that year, had the right kind of snack in the lunchboxes she was providing.

The Exposition was a massive affair, on the scale of a modern Olympics, and attracted visitors from all over the world – and the attention of every caterer in the USA.

Soon advertisements for brownies – of the kind we would recognise today, and nothing to do with pixies – were appearing in newspapers across America, and recipes elaborating on the theme are common in cookbooks on both sides of the Atlantic from the early years of the twentieth century.

The brownie is a brilliant concept: a treat that is at once luxurious and manageable, decadent and compact. The appeal to consumers is obvious, and the appeal to chefs and commercial bakers becomes apparent the moment you start to discuss them.

It is easy to make a tolerably good brownie – my university friends could manage it, and they were half-plastered half the time. It is also easy to store them, package them and transport them, and portion and ingredient control is so straightforward that the theory of brownie production has become a staple of primary school maths lessons – you know: 'Mary has six brownies and gives Joe four. How many does she have left?' Answer, none, because I ate them both.

But the purpose of my trip to Sheffield was to discuss chocolate brownies at an altogether more rarefied level, and the reason I had come to Sheffield was the presence there of Bullion Chocolate – which was where I headed straight from the station.

Bullion – the name riffing on the city's metallic culture – was founded by Max Scotford six years ago, and these days the little firm has a great set-up in the trendy Kelham Island area of the city, where they turn out excellent bars of chocolate... and sensational brownies.

People who make really good chocolate often also make really good brownies, because they have a deep understanding of how the main ingredient works. It's a mistake to think that because chocolate melts easily it must be a cinch to cook with: it can be tricky stuff, and one of the first lessons that cooks who are serious about baking learn is to treat it with care.

One obvious point that escapes many amateurs, and a surprising percentage of professionals, is that if you use rubbish chocolate you are likely to end up with a rubbish cake. It's true that you can achieve pleasing results by melting a Mars Bar and pouring the resulting goo over vanilla ice cream, but far too many people believe that this is a principle that can be applied to all chocolate cookery.

It can't, mainly because mass-market chocolate bars contain a lot more fat and sugar than cocoa solids, and all of this tends to separate and misbehave when exposed to heat, with messy consequences.

Really good pastry chefs use really good chocolate – and if the person making the brownie has also made the chocolate, so much the better.

That certainly applies in the case of Bullion's brownies, which I first encountered when writing a book about British chocolate makers a few years back. They call them Bean-to-Brownies, which reflects the fact that they receive their cocoa at the little factory as beans in sacks, roast and process them and direct some of the finished chocolate into bars... and some into their brownies.

The result is a little square of bliss that preserves the authentic, characteristic flavour of the chocolate – which will vary according to the origin of the beans – and combines it with a texture that hints at crunch, then delivers a satisfying moment of chewiness before melting in the mouth with a final flavour hit.

I have eaten many, many brownies in the name of research, but none – to my mind – quite match Bullion's. So what's the secret? You can find out if you join one of the factory open days that they run most Saturdays, when you can watch Max and the team going about their quasi-magical business before settling down with a brownie and a cuppa. If you get the chance, grill them on their methods.

I certainly grilled Max. How come his brownies are so good? Great ingredients. 'With chocolate and butter being the main make-up of a brownie, it's key that those two ingredients are of exceptional quality,' he told me. 'You can be using the most amazing local butter, but if your chocolate is poor – then the overall bake quality is going to be compromised.'

Bullion is one of only a handful of chocolate makers in this country who perform the whole process – from cocoa bean to chocolate bar – themselves, rather than buying in bulk chocolate and re-melting it. 'Combining that with our local farmers that produce the most amazing dairy products – you know it's a recipe for success,' Max said. But there are two more vital points: 'Timing... baking till just set, for that indulgent fudge-like texture. And don't forget to go heavy on your sea salt – that just takes a humble brownie to another dimension.'

I scored a dozen brownies from Max to take back to family and colleagues down south, knowing that not all of them would survive the journey. Back on the train, I reflected on my flying visit. Everything about Max's brownie felt right, and justified the esteem that this little oblong of squidgy, melting goodness enjoys from all right-thinking Britons. True Slice? I wasn't quite sure. But undoubtedly the fairest square.

Still, I had a sense that this quest was unfulfilled. I needed a chocolate cake that was delicious, and had a story behind it, and expressed an aspect of Britishness... and I needed an appropriate location in which to eat it. Back home, I consulted my keenest cake-fan friends, who all had personal choices, but none that they could argue properly fitted my criteria.

And then the Queen died.

I expect that strange day still lives large in the minds of many of us, and I will never forget the pin-drop silence in the normally frantic newsroom when Huw Edwards appeared in black tie with official confirmation that Elizabeth II had passed away. The *Telegraph*'s offices are two hundred yards along Buckingham Palace Road from the palace itself, and at the end of that long, strange day I walked with colleagues through the crowds, not yet impassable, and right up to the gates, where the first floral tributes were being laid in the darkness as the drizzle turned gradually to torrential rain.

The next few days, as you might expect, were mightily busy in a newspaper office, and I had plenty to do helping to prepare special supplements for the lying-in-state, the processions and the funeral. I wasn't thinking about cake much.

But something must have stuck in my mind, because months later, when I had exhausted almost all avenues in the search for the right chocolate cake, I suddenly remembered something that I had read somewhere amid the stacks of online cuttings about the Queen's chef, and a cake on the train.

A brief but frantic search ensued, and then I found the article in which Darren McGrady, a former chef at Buckingham Palace, recalled a chocolate biscuit cake which he said was 'Her Majesty the Queen's favourite afternoon tea cake by far.'

I thought, with all due respect to her late Majesty: Yessssss.

He continued: 'This cake is probably the only one that is sent into the Royal dining room again and again until it has all gone.'

Bingo.

The former royal chef went on to assert that the monarch was so fond of the cake that he personally – Darren, that is – transported leftovers to her weekend base near London, regularly travelling on the train from London to Windsor Castle with a tin of biscuit cake perched on his knee.

'If there is anything left when she has it at Buckingham Palace, it then goes to Windsor Castle so she can finish it there,' he said. Further research also revealed that this item had been the only other cake, apart from the wedding cake, to have been served at the wedding of the then Duke and Duchess of Cambridge in 2011. Unless this had been at the express request of the groom's grandmother, we may safely assume that chocolate fridge cake – for that is what it was – has a long and assured future at the heart of our national life.

That will do for me, I thought. The only snag was that Darren now plies his trade in Texas, playing up, entirely understandably, his former royal appointment in a manner that clearly goes down a storm with the aristocracy of the Lone Star State.

But Texas is an awfully long way to go to get hold of a slice of cake. So where else can I obtain it?

Fortnum & Mason, despite being grocers and provision merchants to her late Majesty and holding a royal warrant from her successor, do not sell such a cake. Nor does the Buckingham Palace gift shop. Hmmm.

I noodled around on the internet, finding plenty of versions of the recipe (Darren specifies Rich Tea biscuits in the mix, or 'sweet cookies', the latter option surely only for his American audience) but nowhere I might purchase the finished item... the journey to acquire a cake, you will have noticed, being a vital part of the process for me. Then I remembered a visit to a little shop down in the south-west not all that long ago.

It was a family holiday of a few days to Dorset, one of my favourite places in the world. We stayed in Lulworth Cove, which is gorgeously scenic in itself and also a good base for exploring the Jurassic Coast. Not far from Lulworth, on the Isle of Purbeck, is the lovely little self-contained resort town of Swanage, which has all that one can wish for in a seaside destination – and a world-class chocolate shop.

CAKE

I took my daughter Lucy and our dog Sammy along to Swanage for the day, and as well as messing around on the beach, wandering down the pier, checking out a souvenir shop and playing crazy golf, we also stopped by at Chococo, which I knew from a previous visit while working on my book about British chocolate.

The shop and café are not easy to find, down an alley off a back-street close to the station where the heritage steam trains pull in, but it's well worth the 100-metre detour from the sea front.

Chococo was set up by Claire Burnet and her husband Andy twenty years ago to make fine filled chocolates with local ingredients, and other delicious chocolate-related items. These days they have a few other branches, as well as a pristine little chocolate factory, but the Swanage café remains the 'mothership' for all they do, as well as a popular spot with in-the-know locals for tea and treats.

On the day I visited with Lucy we sat outside and enjoyed toasties and chocolate croissants, and I recalled an array of bakes on the counter. Now, I wondered... and looked up their website. 'Classic chocolate biscuit cake. Made with Rich Tea biscuits...' Sold.

Claire kindly sent a note along with the cake, explaining how it came about. 'It is my adaptation of an old family recipe that reminds me of helping my mum make chocolate treats for Christmas,' she wrote. 'We found the original recipe in one of her cookbooks, written in my best twelve-year-old handwriting, and it has been a family favourite ever since! I can fully understand why the late Queen loved chocolate biscuit cakes

248

too and we totally agree with her with regard to preferring rich tea biscuits as they stay satisfyingly crunchy! I also love the addition of dried cherries and raisins for pops of tart sweetness in amongst the rich chocolate crunch. The other joy of this biscuit cake is that it is very easy to make with children. Enjoy!'

My colleagues in the office in Buckingham Palace Road interrupted my reading to suggest that we were surely close enough to the Palace to warrant consumption right there and then.

No, I said. It must be eaten in the right manner, and in the right place.

'*In* Buckingham Palace?'

Er... yes.

'How are you going to manage that? Stride up to the gates and say: "Let me in. I must eat this cake in the Palace"? You'll be banged up. Rightly.'

True. Also, popping round the corner reduces the element of quest to that of jaunt. It lacks nobility.

Whereas recreating the journey of the royal cake-maker and cake-bearer had a much more Arthurian ring to it. Let it be so. I would travel even as the late Queen's devoted servant had travelled, not in a gilded carriage or aboard a prancing steed, but in a single-class commuter train from London Paddington to Windsor & Eton Central (changing at Slough), with the Queen's favourite chocolate cake in a tin on my lap.

A suitably regal tin, of course, and for that the Buckingham Palace gift shop did come in handy. I got a smart oblong tin of their finest Scottish shortbread biscuits, embossed (the tin, not the biscuits) with the royal coat of arms, took it back to the office and distributed the biscuits, which were nothing special, to be honest, among my hungry colleagues, cut myself a couple of slices of Royal Rich Tea Chocolate Fridge Cake, and I was all set.

Fittingly, I took the Elizabeth Line from Paddington to Slough. It might have been quicker to take a main line train, but opening this long-delayed railway had been one of Her Majesty's last public duties, so I was simply adding another level of respect to my journey when I climbed aboard with my cake.

I had done a little further research at home the previous night, and noted that the entry procedures at Windsor Castle involved 'airport-style' security, including X-ray scanners and metal-detecting gates, so regretfully I had left my newly acquired Buckingham Palace biscuit tin at home, and instead concealed my slices of Rich Tea Chocolate Fridge Cake about my person, wrapped in non-PVC clingfilm and a biodegradable bag (a nod to the current, planet-friendly monarch).

The Elizabeth Line took me smoothly to Slough, a town that one of the Queen's Poet Laureates had recommended for destruction by enemy bombers on account of its inhuman ugliness, but one separated from Windsor only by the River Thames and a mile or so of water-meadows.

The two towns are connected by a two-carriage shuttle train every half an hour, and I caught one almost straight away, emerging from Windsor & Eton Central opposite the giant ramparts of the castle.

Moments later I was in the security lobby, noting with relief the absence of pike-wielding Beefeaters but nervous to be told that I had to put my cake-containing coat through the X-Ray machine. Beltless, and breathless with apprehension, I walked through the metal detecting arch and waited on the other side while the lady gazing at the scanner screen took forever to release my coat from its depths. Would the cake show up as a suspicious mass? Would they think it was plastic explosive? Were the dungeons here still operative?

I would not find out, at least for a while. I retrieved my coat and walked up the hill into the castle proper. The cake was already burning a hole in my pocket. Figuratively. Non-figuratively, it was still a couple of degrees below zero after the coldest night of the year, the lawn in front of St George's Chapel was white with frost, and the cake in my pocket had the consistency of iron.

I went to the chapel first, not because I intended to consume any cake there, but to pay my respects and do my best to excuse my forthcoming transgression.

I had arrived soon after opening time, and there were few people in the Chapel apart from the red-caped guides sitting strategically close to ancient radiators and heating ducts. I needn't enumerate the glories of this building or the assorted monarchs entombed there; but I found it beautiful, and fascinating and – as I bowed my head for a moment at the entrance to the late Queen's last resting place – moving.

I lit a candle at a votive spot close to the exit, and mentally asked some higher power and the spirit of our late monarch for forgiveness in advance of minor misbehaviour.

Emerging from the chapel I walked uphill and around the flank of the main building. Below and to the west the meadows and woodlands, and the playing fields of Eton, were a sea of frosty white. At the entrance to the State Apartments stood a soldierly figure and two more guides... but I wasn't searched.

In case of any final obstacle to my plan, any last-minute confiscation or altercation, I first checked out my fallback plan, the Undercroft Café. As I thought: their smartly presented but limited range of cakes included such non-regal interlopers as Red Velvet and Carrot Cake, but no Rich Tea Chocolate Fridge Cake. If I absolutely had to I could stoop to a slice of Victoria sponge, but that would play havoc with my chapter structure... I hoped it wouldn't come to that.

I walked upstairs and followed the red ropes and indications of the guides through the State Apartments, trusting that I would sense the correct moment to reach for my slice.

The Waterloo Chamber was too vast and imposing, though the Georgian Kings hung on its walls certainly looked as if they had been well-disposed towards cake in their lifetimes. The Grand Reception Room beyond lived up to its name and was overwhelming. I then passed, at a stately pace disguising my impatience, through chambers (drawing-room, dining room, closet, etc.) designated King's and therefore unfit for my purpose, before my interest was piqued by the rooms called the Queen's Audience Chamber and, even better, the Queen's Presence Chamber: I fingered the clingfilmed lump in my pocket. I could say that I had eaten the correct cake in the Queen's Presence... Chamber.

But something held me back. The titles were appealing, but I knew that the Queen they referred to was actually Catherine of Braganza, wife of Charles II who remodelled the state rooms, and who was also the lady looking down on me in painted form from the ceiling of the room as I considered my options. Perhaps it was Catherine's disapproving glare, but... no.

In the Garter Throne Room, though, I sensed that my moment had come. For one thing, this was a room that the late Queen Elizabeth had used often and with great pride and pleasure, when investing members of the Order of the Garter, a high honour in her gift: her throne stood at one end of it, and an attractively human portrait of her was placed over the marble fireplace.

More importantly still, the room did not currently contain a guide or guard, perhaps on the basis that there weren't any priceless works of art or craft on display in there, perhaps because one had wandered off for a chat with a pal.

Just in case, I affected an interest in the glass cabinet containing the regalia of the Order of the Garter while I fiddled around in my pocket attempting to free my cake from its wrapper. This was surprisingly difficult, because non-PVC clingfilm is fiendish, and because I couldn't get it out to look at what I was doing without being rumbled and clapped in irons.

At last I had it free, and the coast was still clear. I gave a fake cough and brought my hand to my lips as if to muffle the next one, slipping a fairly hefty chunk of Rich Tea Chocolate Fridge Cake, the True Slice, into my mouth.

Really, a very big chunk. How's it going to look if I choke, I wondered, chewing as discreetly as I could manage. And why did Claire have to include raisins?

The chocolate started to melt, the biscuit gradually dissolved, and a delicious combination of flavours washed over me. I glanced at Her late Majesty Queen Elizabeth II in her portrait by Sir James Gunn, looking back at me from her gilded frame to my left.

I'm not going to say that she nodded in approval. That didn't happen. But I nodded my head at her, with respect... not least for her taste in cake. Perhaps, in time, Her Majesty's son and successor will confer a warrant on his late mother's favourite cake. That would be official confirmation that chocolate fridge cake is to the British what flourless chocolate cake is to the Italians, and the brownie to the USA: a True Slice.

CHOCOCO CHOCOLATE BISCUIT CAKE

The recipe below, kindly given to me by Chococo's founder, Claire Burnet, is for their version of the cake in log form, although you can obviously use any kind of mould you like. If you have important visitors coming – say, the Prince and Princess of Wales – the recipe for the Buckingham Palace version is in an excellent little volume called A Royal Cookbook by Darren McGrady's successor, Mark Flanagan, which includes many fine glossy photographs of the Palace version, glossily swathed in shiny chocolate ganache and further decorated with gilded chocolate buttons modelled, the book declares, with the aid of actual buttons from actual royal footmen.

Whichever version you choose to make, you will need a large, sharp knife to cut it – just don't wave the blade around anywhere near the Prince and Princess, or their bodyguards will shoot you.

You'll need an 18 x 28cm Swiss roll tin or a 22cm square brownie tin, lined with baking parchment.

CAKE

MAKES ONE BIG CAKE, 12 BARS OR 24 MINI 'BITES'

150g Rich Tea biscuits

125g unsalted butter

200g 70–72% dark chocolate

1 tbsp golden caster sugar

2 tbsp golden syrup

125g raisins (or your preferred combination of dried fruit and/or nuts to suit your taste)

50g dried cherries

Topping
200g milk chocolate or dark chocolate, chopped

1. Crush the biscuits into small pieces. The easiest method is to put them into a plastic bag and bash them with a rolling pin, but not too much, you don't want crumbs!
2. Put the butter, dark chocolate, sugar and golden syrup into a large heavy-based pan and set over a low heat. Let melt, stirring continuously.
3. Take off the heat, add the crushed biscuits and fruits and mix well until everything is coated in the chocolate mixture.
4. Pour the mixture into the prepared tin and transfer to the fridge to set.

FOR THE TOPPING

1. Most people overheat chocolate when melting it at home and then wonder why it doesn't set properly or why it sets with big streaks in it. This is because you need to 'temper' the chocolate to get it to the correct crystallisation structure, such that when it sets, it will set properly with a clean snap and will be streak-free! Tempering techniques can get technical and a bit intimidating, but a simple kitchen logic approach that I use for melting chocolate at home is this – when melting chocolate, only ever initially melt about 70% of the total. As soon as this has melted, you need to drop the temperature down quickly as this chocolate will be too hot to work with. You do this by adding the remaining 30% of 'cold' chocolate to melt in. You are aiming to get the temperature down to 28–30°C max. You then gently warm the chocolate back up just a few degrees to get to the ideal working temperature of 33–34°C.

2. Also, another top tip, don't boil a kettle, open your dishwasher or do anything else that will create humidity in your kitchen when working with chocolate!

3. OK, back to preparing your chocolate topping – melt 140g of the chopped chocolate in a heatproof bowl set over a saucepan of barely simmering water. Make sure the water is not touching the bottom of the bowl.

4. When just melted (and no longer), take the bowl off the saucepan, place on a cool surface and add the remaining 60g of chopped chocolate, stirring it gently to melt. Once it has all melted in, pop the bowl back on the saucepan and stir gently for 2 minutes to bring the temperature back up slightly, using the residual heat from the water in the saucepan. If you don't have a thermometer to check the exact temperatures, don't worry too much; if you follow this process you should be in the right ballpark, temperature-wise.

5. Pour the chocolate over the chilled biscuit cake mixture, spreading it over the surface with a metal spatula.

6. Put the biscuit cake back into the fridge or a cool room (ideally at 14°C) until the topping has set; then cut into slices to suit with a hot knife.

7. The biscuit cake will keep stored in an airtight container in the fridge for up to 3 weeks (as if!).

CHAPTER 12
THE *BAKE OFF* SHOWSTOPPER

One of the main reasons for this book's existence, along with nominative determinism and my fondness for sugary snacks, is *The Great British Bake Off*. It is not only that I like to watch it with my family (and on my own if they are not available), it is the way that *Bake Off* has done more than any other single innovation of my lifetime to push baking, and cakes in particular, to a prominent position in the national consciousness.

Why does this show strike such a powerful chord with so many of us? If the ingredients are set out plainly it does not seem a recipe for an irresistible confection: a bumptious baker and an octogenarian expert, two eccentric presenters and a tent. *Game of Thrones* it ain't. Yet it remains, entering its fourteenth series, among the most popular shows on British television, often the most-watched programme on any channel at the time that it airs, and the parent of multiple international offspring, of whom more later.

The *Bake Off* of today is a tremendously slick piece of television, balancing tension and banter, with every element

accorded just the right amount of screen time in an impeccably edited package. Even the adverts seem to have been
incorporated with the minimum of fuss, and the occasional
change of presenter or tweak to the format is achieved without
disturbing the serene and compelling progress of one of the
most firmly established favourites on the nation's televisual
calendar.

Some of the greatest bakes – usually Showstoppers – have
imprinted themselves forever on my memory. I think back
with awe to John Whaite's gingerbread Roman Coliseum in
Series 3; to Nadiya's 'Pouring Soda-Can' cheesecake tower in
Series 6; Kim-Joy's turtle-filled Galaxy chocolate ball in Series
9… there are so many others, each more bonkers than the
last.

These insane set-pieces, intended to demonstrate the extent
of the bakers' skills and the outer reaches of their imagina-
tions, not only grip television viewers but set social media
alight. They have had a traumatic effect on many home bakers,
especially those who watch the show with their families. What
is the point of coming up with a Victoria sandwich for your
children's birthday party when they have just seen a staircase
of eclairs, or a fully functioning, yet fully cake, windmill?

The showstoppers are the epitome of what the cake has
become in the twenty-first century: a focus for fun and family,
as ever, but also a technological marvel and a globally accessible career calling-card. What would a Saxon swineherd's wife
make of it?

More to the point, how could I engage with it? How could
I come across a True Slice that was relevant to *Bake Off*?

You can't buy a Showstopper – they're not commercially available, or at least not on my budget. Could I make my own? I didn't see how. It was a major dilemma. I knuckled down to some *Bake Off* history, hoping that a solution would materialise.

The show's success was far from instant. To begin with, it took years – four years, in fact – for the programme's creators, Richard McKerrow and Anna Beattie of Love Productions, to persuade any major channel that their idea was worth commissioning.

With hindsight that seems hard to believe, but if you imagine a world in which *Bake Off* did not exist, who would think it should? Baking is fun, if you're the one doing it, but have you ever sat at home and watched someone else bake? For long?

Most of the process is waiting for the oven to do its work, which is why the banter of the presenters, the cutaways to local wildlife and the dozens of little mini-cliffhangers all need to be edited together to maintain momentum and tension which is often lacking in real life.

Some of the anxieties of the editors who eventually commissioned the show for BBC2 (note, not BBC1) showed in the first series, which was quite literally all over the place.

They decided that the *Bake Off* tent, a conscious echo of the village fête which had been a key inspiration, should be lugged around the country to locations of questionable relevance to the baking theme of the week (I am aware that the guiding philosophy of this book is similar. But they went, for example, to Sandwich in Kent for Bread Week, which seems desperate even by my standards). And there were mini lectures from the resident experts, Paul Hollywood and Mary Berry, on the different varieties of baking that were being showcased.

Mel Giedroyc and Sue Perkins, the original presenting pair, were terrific right from the start, with an instinctive grasp of the right blend of sauciness and seriousness, and a chemistry born of years of collaboration. But still it all seemed a little clunky, and viewers and reviewers were somewhat bewildered.

Soon, though, it became apparent that Love Productions and BBC2 were on to a winner, and the midweek slot, often up against Champions League football, started to deliver impressive ratings, and a genuine dilemma for sports fans who also loved to bake – or loved to watch people fail to bake.

The winner of the first season was Edd Kimber, who has gone on to a highly successful career as a cookbook author, lecturer and demonstrator – as have most of his successors – while the show settled into its format, found a permanent base, became less didactic and more fun – and spawned a clutch of offspring around the world.

Thirty-five countries now make their own versions of the show, from Finland (*Koko Suomi Leipoo* – 'All Finland Bakes') to Australia, where the setting is a shed rather than a tent. Among the latest versions to air are those from Mexico, Uruguay and Morocco, where the series premiere achieved a remarkable 40% audience share. Versions of the programme now air in more than 200 countries, with keen fans seeking out exotic iterations online; in a closing of the circle, it's rumoured that Channel 4 are looking to air *The Great Australian Bake Off* on prime time British TV – which would make sense, as one of the judges is Croydon-born cooking star Rachel Khoo.

Some people have suggested that the series presents a soft-focus, inaccurately cuddly face of Britain to the world, with hints of the vicarage lawn and the village fête and an extraordinary amount of hugging.

It certainly perpetuates ancient tropes carried over from the *Carry On* films of the Sixties and Seventies, and based on the kind of words that provoke back-of-the-class giggles: firm and fruity, soft and springy, moist and yielding – sometimes the show tiptoes around a swamp of double entendres, and the co-presenters rarely have to work very hard to raise a giggle from the competitors with a suggestive remark about a failure to rise.

All of this is surely tied up with the notion that in the British mind a cake is somehow ever so slightly wicked or transgressive, representative of some kind of moral lapse, forgiveable evidence of human frailty in the face of temptation or, as the future novelist Salman Rushdie put it when writing copy about cream cakes for the advertising agency Ogilvy & Mather, they are 'Naughty, but nice'.

If *GBBO* were the only programme conceived in this country that was ever broadcast abroad that might perhaps be an issue, but it seems to me that the feel-good *Bake Off* is at worst a balancing positive element in an export industry that also includes the relentlessly grim *Peaky Blinders*, *Silent Witness* and *Line of Duty*.

It is not as if the tent is ever entirely free from drama, conflict and jeopardy: there was a notorious incident of custard theft in Series 4; Prue Leith accidentally announced the winner of the 2017 contest too early on social media; and the entire show decamped from the BBC to Channel 4 in 2016, taking only Paul Hollywood along from the original presenting team.

Yet for all the international fame, tabloid headlines and high-stakes contractual manoeuvring, the show retains a powerful charm, in part I think because it tacitly invites viewers to imagine themselves as bakers. Even the frequent celebrity specials emphasise the fallibility of the rich and famous, so that while watching at home we can't help thinking: 'Oh my goodness, that sponge is collapsing and/or that meringue is tragic. What would I do to fix it?'

My favourite *GBBO* dialogue, which completely cracked me up when shown live and has since become a popular internet meme, comes from a recent celebrity special in which Paul Hollywood subjected an unfortunate stand-up comedian to a blue-eyed interrogation over a baking tray draped with tragic little failures.

> *Hollywood: 'Tell us about your flapjacks?'*
> *James Acaster: 'Started to make them. Had a breakdown.*
> *Bon appétit.'*

To be perfectly honest I can spend hours lost on YouTube watching out-takes from the hundreds of shows and celebrity specials that have aired down the years. There are countless videos devoted only to disasters: sliced fingers, topless pies, warm ice cream; competitors weeping, screaming, silent with sheer disbelief at the depth of their own incompetence. But I prefer the compilations that include moments of joy and congratulation as well as catastrophe; they're such a concentrated hit of the highs and lows of human existence, like Kipling's lines about triumph and disaster but much more entertaining. That's Kipling the poet, by the way, not Kipling the imaginary cake-maker.

Recently, cunning entertainment entrepreneurs focused on the high street rather than the small screen have realised that this appeal is highly marketable, and come up with events that allow members of the public to find out for themselves just how difficult it is to bake against the clock in a tent, mimicking many aspects of the programme while steering carefully clear of any trademarked elements and not employing any of the contracted celebrities.

Like millions of others I love to watch *Bake Off* at home en famille, debating without too much rancour or malice which contestants we feel are most likely to survive each week, and pronouncing with confident superiority on technical errors, tactical blunders and shocking aesthetic howlers.

I didn't realise that my confidence could be tested in real life until my elder daughter pointed out the existence of these *Bake-Off*-alike evenings, noted their proximity to our home, mentioned that she had long wanted to take part in one and asserted, with justification, the suitability of such an evening for inclusion in my book.

In other words, she had found the solution to my dilemma. I felt like Cinderella: You SHALL bake a Showstopper! And before you could say spatula we were on the correct website and booking an evening's competitive baking in a tent in Haggerston, in the very far east of London.

The Big Bakes don't make it abundantly clear on their website that they have nothing officially to do in any way with *The Great British Bake Off*, so I am going to do it for them – there is no formal relationship between the two: it is just that the format that the Big Bakes have chosen for their events bears more than a passing resemblance to a certain popular competitive baking show. There are experts to encourage and judge the results, there are bakers at individual workstations, and there is a tent.

A very fine tent. All that Lucy and me had to do was get to it. Ordinarily this would be no problem at all, since the Big Bakes' east London venue is just over the road from Haggerston station on the London Overground train network.

Unfortunately our evening's baking coincided with a national rail strike, so we had to drive across London, enduring jams and navigational nightmares that raised our stress levels to maximum before we had caught sight of so much as a balloon whisk. The journey would subsequently prove to have cost me two separate fines for obscure traffic transgressions.

Clearly, the Big Bake was not the easiest of places to find. No doubt deliberately, it doesn't advertise its operation to passers-by, and those who have signed up for an evening's competitive baking and followed the directions encounter (after, in our case, driving around the block a couple of times) a glass door under a railway bridge leading into what seems to be a modestly sized bakery store room – sacks of flour, bins, tea towels – with three substantial fridge doors at the rear. One of these opened, after investigation, into a baking-themed cocktail bar, where the evening's participants were assembling.

This in itself offered ample evidence of the way that baking, and *Bake Off*, have become a big part of mainstream culture, no longer simply a household necessity or the preserve of highly qualified professionals, but a vehicle for a wild and crazy night out, fuelled by high-octane, palate-challenging combos such as the bright pink bakewelltini.

Or, in our case, Diet Cokes, which we took out to a terrace outside the bar, to admire a most extraordinary sight.

There, in a yard hemmed in by high walls, the kind of territory traditionally occupied in this part of east London by a car breaker's yard, was a replica of the televised *Bake Off*'s tent, glowing from within and looking like some kind of recently landed culinary spaceship.

Sophia, the host of the evening, a young woman of about Lucy's age – mid-twenties – showed us to our bake station, which was prepped with ingredients. We'd pre-ordered themed chef's toques and logo-bedecked aprons, because I am a profligate idiot. Our fellow bakers were three couples, two pairs maybe in their late twenties and one maybe late thirties, all on what seemed to be date nights and none wearing themed baking gear.

But there was no time for self-consciousness. Sophia rattled through basic instructions – what we had at our bake stations (oven, hob, stand mixer, pots, pans, implements and ingredients), location of extra ingredients, fridges, cooling racks, hand-washing area and loos.

'You have eighty minutes!' she cried, channelling her celebrity counterparts. 'Get baking!'

We looked at the instructions on the sheet on our prep surface, and I realised at once a fundamental difference between our programme and that watched by millions on Wednesdays.

On the televised *Bake Off*, the competitors are there to entertain the audience with their baking skills, or lack of same. Here in Haggerston, the baking was the entertainment, and we only had to amuse ourselves.

The recipe was for a Geometric Jewel Cake. Hmm, I thought, that's...

'It's a smash cake,' Lucy declared.

'A...?'

'Smash cake. Chocolate shell. Cake inside. Actually –' she scanned down the recipe card – 'cake pop inside.'

'What?'

'Smooshed-up cake. In a chocolate shell. Come on. What are you waiting for? Clock's ticking.'

You'll have noticed, dear reader, that this book is far from being a how-to manual. I admitted very early on that when it comes to baking I am no more than a keen amateur, and I see it as no part of my role to provide step-by-step guidance on the cakes I am describing, leaving that for the recipe at the end of each chapter.

So I'm not going to describe every moment of our Haggerston bake here, and if you want the instructions (which are very, very easy) you can skip to the end of the chapter.

Anyhow, Lucy – who had baked up a storm during lockdown, often collaborating on gluten-free delights with her coeliac sister Emily – took charge, and I was happy to do as I was told.

Our expert, Sophia, charged around in a jolly manner, making sure that everyone was happy with their kit and ingredients, not issuing instructions but happy to be consulted if required; meanwhile trains pulled in and out of the station almost above our heads, and a soundtrack provided a seamless succession of Noughties disco bangers.

It was an upbeat, all-action, good-humoured process. The recipe had obviously been reverse-engineered to fit the timescale available with just a little bit of wriggle-room in hand, and the process was almost entirely idiot-proof, or as far as that is possible when elements such as raw eggs and actual heat are involved.

Not entirely idiot-proof, it transpired. First of all I had barely started to whisk our sponge batter when the whisk came to pieces in my hands, to the amusement of the couple at the next bake station – a technical failure and not my fault, as I made clear at some volume. But not a good look either.

We successfully baked a sponge (despite the fact that I set the timer on my phone but did not actually start it) and made a Swiss meringue buttercream, which tasted sumptuous and looked highly convincing, forming the celebrated soft peaks in the mixer bowl that suggested that it would make splendid meringues.

We raided the shelves in the corner of the tent for spices and flavourings: chai and vanilla for the sponge, orange essence for the buttercream – a combination that Sophia, who was evidently not there to give her guests unconditional praise, considered 'pretty good', while we had been hoping for 'Wow, amazing!'

Following the instruction sheet we then – slightly disappointingly, I felt – crumbled our sponge and smooshed it together with the buttercream into a kind of brown putty, rather than making an elegant frosted sandwich cake. For reasons that I entirely understood, the recipe we had been set was pitched at the most undemanding end of the talent scale: any terrible mistakes could be smothered in chocolate and presented to the judge with a straight face: more of a gobstopper than a Showstopper. But there was no time for reflection.

The two younger couples were exchanging lingering glances between baking steps, while the thirties pair seemed to be putting away a fair bit of liquor. Lucy and I buzzed happily around ticking off the steps, feeling almost competent and only enjoyably stressed.

I melted some dark chocolate and Lucy lined an elaborate latex mould with it, then, after it had chilled, gently rammed the smooshy mixture into it before I sealed what would become the base with another layer of dark chocolate.

We plonked it back into the freezer to set the base a full 90 seconds before Sophia bellowed that 'One minute remains, bakers, one minute!' and we felt very smug when she called time while the tipsy couple were still flailing around with molten chocolate and sugar sprinkles.

Lucy trotted up to the judging table with our cake, which she had latterly splattered with a Jackson Pollock arc of melted white chocolate.

The contestants gathered around, and Sophia, who for all her youth was admirably fluent and diplomatic, found something to praise in each creation, having gently quizzed the practitioners about their flavour and topping choices. The 'winners' were one of the late twenties couples, on what turned out to be a birthday outing. Sophia may conceivably have been tipped off about this... or perhaps I am bitter that we were not the winners, because I had found myself quite carried away with the competitive process while we were cooking.

The evening reminded me that baking can be great fun, that baking with family members only adds to the fun – and that baking a cake, much more than simply choosing a cake – brings certain personality traits to the surface.

Lucy, for example, is a perfectionist who cares deeply about the flavour of any food she is cooking, and was constantly tasting and adjusting as we cooked; whereas I – the victim of a lifetime in newsrooms – am always more concerned about deadlines and delivery, and made sure that we were (pointlessly) ahead of our rivals at every stage, to no beneficial effect on our final product.

Sophia had cut a corner of our cake to judge the interior, but she politely squidged it back on so that we proudly produced an almost immaculate cake from our souvenir cardboard box when we arrived home later that night. My wife obviously needed to taste a slice, and pronounced it 'not bad, but a bit heavy on the chocolate', and Lucy immediately awarded herself a slice which she devoured with a slug of plant-based cream – the vital finishing touch, apparently.

But it didn't seem to me either the time or the place to tackle a slice and declare it True. For one thing, it *was* a bit heavy on the chocolate, and, delicate flower that I am, I find that dark chocolate last thing at night prevents me from sleeping.

For another thing, I had a cunning plan.

Keen viewers of *GBBO* on television will have noted that the tent is not, in fact, located in a railway yard in a dodgy area of east London, but in the beautiful grounds of an elegant country house somewhere in England.

I had assumed, like many viewers, that this was a hotel only too delighted to accommodate the bakers and their crew and which no doubt did a roaring trade in fans keen to stay close to the scene of the action.

All I had to do, I thought, was to book myself into said hotel and I would be ideally placed to consume my True Slice of self-manufactured Big Bake cake.

As usual with my cake plans, however, things were not so straightforward: the main problem being that the vast, classy, stately building in whose grounds the *Bake Off* tent is erected is not in fact a hotel at all, but someone's actual home.

Blast.

What were the chances, I wondered, of a warm reception if I simply showed up at Welford Park in Berkshire, the stately pile in question, with a slice of my smash cake and asked to be admitted in order to consume it?

I anticipated an adverse reaction. Then I discovered that the owners of Welford Park, the Puxleys, descendants of the family who bought it the one and only time the manor changed hands for money, in 1618, are very proud of the snowdrops in the grounds. So proud that they allow the public in to view these pretty little flowers on a few days of the year in the brief snow-drop season in February and March.

By happy chance it was early in the year when I found out about this, and by happier chance Welford is ten minutes down the road from my mother's village, so I was able to combine a visit to her – to present her with a slice of the cake baked by her son and granddaughter – with a visit to Welford Park, to eat a slice of that cake on the site of the *Bake Off* tent.

I mean, of course, to examine their lovely snowdrops.

Nothing to do with cake at all.

It's interesting, from a sociological point of view, that *GBBO* started out as an itinerant show, and the original reason for setting it in a tent was so that the entire set-up could be packed up and shifted around the country at the end of each episode. The notion that this oddball team could show up in a car park near you at any time was democratic and endearing: the show belonged to everyone, and no one was safe.

But when it settled, it did so not in a marketplace in middle England or on the municipal playing fields of a nameless conurbation, but on the croquet lawn of a stately home.

Not, it should be noted, the kind of publicly accessible stately home, an English Heritage or National Trust pile, that is beloved by the gently improving and educational *Antiques Roadshow*, but a private house not generally open to the public and one, furthermore, that has passed by family descent for many generations. There's no point looking up Welford Hall on one of those property sites that tell you how much it fetched the last time it changed hands: this place hasn't been on the market since the seventeenth century.

This is the setting that *Bake Off*'s producers decided was correct for their show: one that suggests that the tent and its jolly companions are there by kind permission of the landed gentry; something of the flavour of a village fête in the works of P. G. Wodehouse, where the vicar will open proceedings by thanking the Squire for lending his lawn, and Bertie Wooster will end up with a soggy bottom.

There's nothing sinister about this choice: *Bake Off* may be solidly middle-class, but it is inclusive and diverse, and the presenting team has always been accessible rather than posh. No one is suggesting that baking is something that only snooty folk do, or that the bakers are present on the big house lawn on sufferance.

It seems likeliest that the location was chosen mainly on aesthetic grounds: the best place for a marquee is a lawn, so why not make it an exceptionally pretty lawn? A lawn implies a house, so why not make it an attractive house? And since the show is being sold abroad, why not make it a house that conforms to foreign perceptions of traditional English life – the kind of house, in fact, to which Mr Darcy might retire to change out of his wet shirt?

And it helps the televisual grammar of the show that when it is time to cut away from the tensions of the tent for a breath of fresh air there are so many verdant vistas and cute wild animals on hand.

There's no questioning the beauty of the surroundings. Indeed Welford Park has been inviting the public to share these beauties, on a strictly limited and seasonal basis, for a good many years.

Which was very handy for me, because otherwise I should have had not the slightest chance of any *GBBO*-related valida- tion for my chocolate smash cake.

There is no short cut to becoming a competitor on the show unless you are a celebrity, and I'm not. As a member of the public, the route involves compliance with a twenty-four-point schedule of requirements simply to submit an initial applica- tion, and then a series of auditions and interviews whose potential severity can only be imagined, because they are hedged about with demands for secrecy.

Besides, by the time I got around to looking it up, applica- tions for the current year had closed.

So if I couldn't get into the actual tent on the basis of talent or fame, my best bet was to take my cake to the site of the tent, and for this purpose a snowdrop-related open day at Welford Park was ideal.

I popped a couple of clingfilm-wrapped slices of the choc smash cake into my coat pocket and set off, a little nervously.

What if entry to the Snowdrop Day required some kind of specialist knowledge? It would be a shame if, having found a way around my baking inadequacies, I was to be tripped up by ignorance of hardy perennials.

And if I managed to get in, how would I be able to parlay my deceitful interest in winter-flowering plants into access to the croquet lawn? Do snowdrops grow on croquet lawns? And what if the croquet lawn was in some sequestered part of the grounds, accessible only by members of the family and guarded by fierce, slavering hounds?

I got in; I paid the admission fee, which undoubtedly helped, and I said, 'Nice day for looking at snowdrops!' to the gateman; and then I followed the little signposts that said 'Snowdrops' while also noting grimly those that said 'Please keep off the grass'.

I followed the woodchipped pathways through the woods, which were ravishingly pretty, even a snowdrop agnostic would admit, and the trail led eventually down a long avenue beside the River Lambourn, a vigorous and substantial chalk stream, back towards the huge, handsome house.

Careful reviewing of the relevant long-shots in recorded *Bake Off* episodes had taught me where to look for the tent site in relation to the house, and where the path gave way to the lawn and visitors were directed to the right towards the formal garden or straight on to the tea tent, to the left was a croquet lawn, and clearly distinguishable upon that lawn, the shape of the base of the *Bake Off* tent.

I felt like an archaeologist who has detected the site of an ancient palace by interpreting crop marks from the air.

There on the lawn, which was approached down a shallow set of steps, the tent had left a green impression: clearly, where the floor of the tent – and all those cookers – had weighed down the grass during the few weeks of filming of the last season, the grass had subsequently grown back stronger, so that the shape of the tent stood out against the surroundings.

That meant that it was relatively easy to work out where the judging bench must have stood, and where, therefore, I needed to stand to taste my Big Bake Showstopper slice.

I glanced around for guard dogs, and seeing none I scuttled off the path, down the steps and on to the croquet lawn, feeling in my pocket to release a slice of choc smash cake.

I popped it into my mouth, and recalled Sophia's words of judgement: 'Excellent texture, fine flavours... but a little heavy-handed with the chocolate. Good effort.'

Not a winner, though. And had Prue and Paul been present, they would no doubt have been much more censorious. But in Haggerston I had experienced a shadow of what the real competitors go through, and here on the shadow of the tent I had communed with the absent tutelary spirits of the show. I had done my *Bake Off* bit.

After that moment of communion on the croquet lawn, there seemed little need to keep up my fabricated interest in snowdrops, so I made for the tea tent and souvenir shop, hoping to pick up a *GBBO* tea-towel, perhaps, a commemorative Victoria sponge or a 'Paul Hollywood Shook My Hand' T-shirt.

But there was nothing of the sort. Zilch. Nada.

In the tea tent – not the *Bake Off* tent, and set up in any case next to the loos – ladies were serving hot quiches and the like, and slices of perfectly acceptable-looking cake (ginger, banana, carrot) but none of it made by former winners.

On the sides of the tent were displayed not cast photographs, but certificates and cuttings commemorating the truly impressive amounts raised for charity by previous Snowdrop Days.

And in the gift shop, which seemed to me to be a not entirely converted boot room, there was a lot of quite civilised snowdrop memorabilia, some actual snowdrops (I bought half a dozen, for form's sake) and some jars of Welford Park fruit jelly.

Not the slightest sign anywhere to be seen suggesting any kind of relationship whatsoever with the *Great British Bake Off.* If it hadn't been for that unmistakable shadow on the lawn, I would have doubted the connection myself.

It was all very mysterious. Had I come across a member of the family who own the place – an actual Puxley – I might have asked them, 'Why so shy?' but I was not carrying a Toffometer, and I saw no one wearing a name-tag that said Lord of the Manor, so one can only guess at the reasons for the reticence.

I would have thought that if one is prepared to open one's grounds to the great unwashed in order to raise money for worthy causes, one might attract greater numbers if one advertised one's connection with one of the top-rated shows on national television.

But perhaps for health and safety reasons, or to protect the snowdrops from trampling, the owners don't wish to attract larger crowds. Perhaps, in the same way that people of a certain class used to disdain any social acquaintance with people involved in trade, it is simply not the done thing to admit that one relies to some extent for income on a television programme.

Or perhaps, and given the hefty emphasis on discretion in the terms and conditions for would-be contestants applying to *GBBO*, it is part of the agreement between Welford Park and Love Productions that the former make no public acknowledgement of their association with the latter.

Out of respect for this attitude, I resisted the urge on the way out to dance around on the croquet lawn yelling, 'Prue Leith stood HERE!' If they wish to keep their relationship with *Bake Off* quiet, that is fine and their secret is safe with me.

And you, obviously. Hush!

GEOMETRIC JEWEL CAKE, AS BAKED IN HAGGERSTON

This is based on the instruction sheet that Lucy and I worked from in the tent. I have trimmed down the method but tried to preserve something of the jolly any-twit-can-do-this tone of the recipe.

It is long – perhaps needlessly so, for anyone with half an idea about cake making – but highly explanatory and well pitched for baking novices. Quite a lot of exclamation marks, though...

You will need a geometric heart-shaped mould about 23cm in diameter and 6cm at the deepest point, and a lipped baking tray about 38 x 28cm.

'A geometric chocolate heart filled with a sponge and Swiss meringue cake pop mix and decorated to your heart's content!'

thebigbakes.com

Cake

100g butter

2 eggs

180g caster sugar

130g milk

180g plain flour, mixed with1 tsp baking powder and1 tsp bicarbonate of soda

Buttercream

75g egg whites

150g caster sugar

190g butter

Chocolate shell

200g chocolate of your choice

SPONGE

1. Preheat your oven to 180°C/350°F/Gas Mark 4.
2. First, grab the ingredients for your sponge. Put the butter into your saucepan and place on the hob on a low-medium heat until the butter is fully melted. Stir.
3. Meanwhile, crack your 2 eggs into your mixing bowl, add the sugar to the eggs and whisk using a hand whisk/electric whisk until well combined.
4. Once the butter is melted, remove from the heat and pour in the milk. Then, pour the butter and milk mixture into your mixing bowl with the eggs and

sugar. Whisk to combine, then add the flour, baking powder and bicarbonate of soda and mix to combine.

5. It's time to choose your flavourings! You can add liquid extracts, powder flavours, funfetti sprinkles or grab a citrus fruit to zest. If you want to add food colouring, now is the time!

6. Line your lipped baking tray with baking paper; there is no need to grease the tin or the paper. Pour all the cake batter on to the lined tray and use your spatula to spread it out evenly. Place your cake in the oven and bake for 15–17 minutes. Don't forget to set a timer! The cake should be golden brown in colour and when a skewer is inserted at an angle it should come out clean, meaning your cake is ready. Once baked, transfer to your wire rack, gently peel off the parchment paper to release the steam and allow your cake to cool.

CHOCOLATE SHELL

1. Grab your chosen chocolate (if you want to colour your chocolate, then choose white chocolate and use an oil-based colouring).

2. Grab your saucepan and add your chocolate; place on the hob on a low heat and stir constantly until chocolate has melted. Make sure you don't burn your chocolate! Alternatively melt your chocolate in the microwave in a microwave-suitable bowl in 30-second bursts until melted.

3. Once your chocolate has melted, grab your geometric heart-shaped mould and pour in three-quarters of your chocolate. Grab your pastry brush and begin to spread the melted chocolate inside the mould until it is fully covered. Make sure there are no gaps in your mould. Hold the mould in your hands and move the chocolate around to help it spread evenly. If there are gaps, this could cause it to break when popping your shell out of the mould!

4. Once your mould is covered with chocolate, pour all excess chocolate back into your pan/bowl that it was melted in and set aside. This will be re-melted and used later on to seal your jewel cake!

5. If you have any spillages over the side of your mould, grab a palette knife and scrape the edges to neaten up your mould. This will also help with releasing your cake later on.

6. Once you are happy with your mould, place it in the fridge to set! While your chocolate shell is setting, move on to your Swiss meringue buttercream!

MERINGUE BUTTERCREAM

1. Put the egg whites and sugar into a clean saucepan. Mix together with a silicone spatula/wooden spoon until well combined, then turn the hob to a medium heat and stir slowly and continuously for roughly 4 minutes until the sugar grains are dissolved (rub

some of the mixture between your fingers; if you don't feel any sugar grains, it's ready!).

2. After 4 minutes, or once the sugar is fully dissolved, pour the mixture into your clean mixing bowl. Using a stand mixer or electric whisk, mix for roughly 10 minutes on the max speed. The whisk will incorporate tiny air bubbles, turning the mixture into fluffy white meringue. While you wait, cut your butter into small chunks for the next stage.

3. Once your meringue has stiff peaks (holds its shape when you lift the whisk out the mixture), decrease to a medium speed and carefully start to add the butter one piece at a time – this should take a few minutes. Once all the butter is added, mix for 1 minute on a low speed. Then increase the speed to max and keep mixing until your buttercream is smooth and silky – this will take at least 7 minutes. Don't worry if it curdles early on – it will come together!

4. Once your buttercream is ready, it's time to add your flavourings! Liquid extracts and powdered flavourings are great, but please note if you add cocoa powder, you won't be able to colour over it!

ASSEMBLY

1. It's time to bring all your elements together! You may want to use gloves for this. Grab your sheet of cake and using your hands, begin to crumble it up into a mixing bowl.

2. Once your cake is all crumbled, add a spoon of buttercream at a time and begin mixing your sponge crumbs with your buttercream. You may not need all of the buttercream. It needs to be 'cake pop' consistency, which means the cake mix should shape into a ball and will stay as a ball, we don't want any crumby cake mixture!

3. Once your 'cake pop' mixture is ready, remove your set chocolate mould from the fridge and begin to gently press your mixture into the mould. If you are too forceful you may crack your chocolate mould and it may come out in pieces!

4. You want to fill the mould almost to the top, but leave a little bit of space to seal your jewel cake with your remaining melted chocolate.

5. Once your mould is filled, pop your chocolate pan back on a low heat to gently melt your remaining chocolate (or re-melt in the microwave in 20-second intervals).

6. Once your chocolate has melted, pour this on to your mould over your cake mix and spread evenly with a palette knife to seal the underneath of your cake.

7. Scrape off all excess chocolate to ensure the top is neat and level.

8. Place back in the fridge/freezer for 5–10 minutes, until set.

9. Once your final layer of chocolate is set, remove from the fridge/freezer and grab your cake board/plate. Flip your jewel cake upside down (mould side up)

and begin to gently and slowly peel the edges away from your cake to release.

10. Once your cake has been removed from the mould, it's time to decorate!

11. If you have any excess chocolate, you can use this to drizzle on your chocolate heart and use as a glue to stick your sprinkles and decorations to it.

12. Your Geometric Jewel Cake is now complete!

CHAPTER 13
BACK HOME: HONEY CAKE

I started this book by recalling my first experiences of cake – well, rusks – in my childhood home, and I want to close the book at home, with a cake that often concludes family meals, and which has been present in one form or another at the family meals of different civilisations for many centuries: honey cake.

I can explore this topic without travelling. Not because I am weary of cake quests – who would be? – but because I am fortunate to live at a nexus of honey cake creativity: Maida Vale in central London, an unglamorous spot beside the Edgware Road. Like any square mile in this city, it is multicultural, and the three cultures that are relevant to this chapter are Jewish, for many years strongly established in St John's Wood, just to the west of where I type these words; Russian, represented by many wealthy households in the Wood and Vale; and Mediterranean, common to the many family businesses running south from where I live along the road to Hyde Park Corner. The area is a crossroads both literal and metaphorical, where honey cakes of entirely different kinds from entirely different cultures are sold in the same shops and devoured in the same cafés and restaurants: Honey Cake Central, you might say.

All three have distinctive takes on the honey cake, and I can obtain delicious examples of the trio, as well as sub-variations on all three, by walking no more than ten minutes from my house. Actually, I may find that I have to take a cake break several times while composing the next few pages.

Honey cake is a non-British cake that perfectly reflects multicultural Britain. It's a cake that is not from my home country but is served all the time in my home. It expresses distant cultures but I can find it on my doorstep.

Telling the story of honey cake, therefore, requires very little in the way of actual travel, but I compensate in temporal terms because in order to recount it I need to go far back in time – much further, in fact, than the Anglo-Saxon hearth cakes of my first chapter.

That's because honey cake is one of the very first forms of cake in recorded history, and recorded history goes back a great deal further elsewhere than it does in this country. One of the oldest recipes of any kind, and as far as I can tell the oldest for anything that can remotely be described as cake, comes from the tomb of an Egyptian official called Rekhmire, which dates from the fifteenth century BCE, which is to say about 3,500 years ago.

A painting in his tomb shows Rekhmire, who was the governor of the city of Thebes, being attended and waited upon by servants, some of whom are preparing sacrifices on his behalf.

Some of them are pounding tiger nuts, the tubers of *Cyperus esculentus* (nowadays often regarded as a weed), into some kind of flour, then sifting it and mixing it with a liquid which (because of depictions of honeycombs nearby) experts believe to be honey. The resulting goo is then formed into cone-shaped cakes.

These cakes were intended to please the god Amun, but they would have been perfectly edible – the ancient Egyptians used tiger nuts in all sorts of recipes, and they are likely to have used honey not only for its sweetness but also for its obvious properties as a preservative; it's obviously a good thing for cakes intended to accompany someone on a journey into the afterlife to have a lengthy shelf life.

Centuries after the Egyptians, the ancient Greeks were mad keen on honey cakes, not only as offerings to their gods but also, as noted by Homer, as welcoming gifts to visitors to the household.

There is a wealth of evidence for ancient Roman honey cakes, not least wall-paintings in the buried city of Pompeii and entirely practical recipes for cakes of honey, spelt grains and nuts from the works of the prolific first-century gourmet Apicius.

These are not so very different from the first documented Jewish honey cakes, which are essentially challah bread – made with a dough enriched with eggs and oil – with added honey. According to the *Encyclopedia of Jewish Food*, this version of honey cake, which is associated with the Ashkenazi branch of Judaism based in northern Europe, was first recorded in 1105.

These cakes are the ancestors of one kind of honey cake often eaten in my household, the version known in Yiddish as lekach; the other popular variety is the Russian version known as medovik, which is less Jewish but still very London. The third honey cake in the area is the baklawa/baklava of Mediterranean and Arabic extraction.

The Jewish connection is my wife and – since Judaism passes through the female line – my daughters. My wife descends from Jews who settled in Germany, so the culinary influences of my in-laws mostly reflect Ashkenazi Jewish cooking traditions, more basic, or at any rate less exotic, than the Middle Eastern Sephardic Jewish cuisine.

London's Jewish community mingles those of many heritages, like the wider city itself, and the cookery that results is often a blend of many influences – a kosher melting pot, if you like. My meat-and-two-veg Anglo-Saxon C. of E. heritage can seem dull by comparison with the feasts of the other side of the family, but over nearly three decades I have learned to enjoy everything I am given, learned the importance of always accepting second helpings, and even learned to cook some of the less demanding dishes.

Honey cake, though, I buy, not least because some of my wife's family are more kosher than others, and it is better to be able to tell your guests, 'The cake came from so-and-so's,' thus establishing its credentials, rather than to say that you made it yourself, using who-knows-what ingredients.

Our honey cake is often baked and gifted by a relative (such as my cousin-in-law Lisa Dangoor, whose recipe closes the chapter), or else it comes from Panzer's – of course it does, because we live relatively close to St John's Wood, where there is a thriving Jewish community, and Panzer's food store has been an institution on St John's Wood High Street for many decades.

It is much shinier and slicker than it was when I first visited in the 1980s, when the floor was lino, the shelving was somewhat haphazard and our shopping was recorded in an account book by Peter the owner at the back of the shop – and if rather too much was owing, the ledger clerk in the back room would call out to us to settle up.

Nowadays it is all sparkling clean, chiller cabinets and stainless steel racks under bright lighting, but there is the same cornucopia of Middle Eastern and central European specialities in bright packaging, some kosher, some not... a skilled filleter dispensing smoked salmon to order, and the lekach honey cakes made, as they have been for years, to a recipe from a local lady, Hanna Geller Goldsmith. On her blog, *Building Feasts*, Hanna happily admits that her honey cake recipe is not original (it's hard to see how any recipe for such a fundamental dish could be) but adapted from a recipe of her neighbour's mother, which contains the secret ingredient which renders the cake not only moist (unlike many honey cakes) but delectably sticky: golden syrup.

It's not a golden syrup cake – that would be some kind of heresy – but there is golden syrup involved... as well as honey, of course.

The lekach supposedly gained its name in the Middle Ages – it was first recorded as such in what is now Germany in 1200. The word came into Yiddish, like many other elements of that wonderfully expressive language, from Low German, in which the word lecke means lick (English borrowed it too).

The traditional explanation is that boys entering Hebrew classes would be handed a slate on which the characters had been written and then smeared with honey, so that in licking off the honey they were learning their letters, consuming wisdom.

This sounds peculiar, but surely reflects the importance of honey in Jewish culture, which runs very deep. It is a metaphor throughout the Torah and sometimes represents the texts themselves: in eating honey one is consuming sweet holy knowledge to nourish the inner being. As the book of Ezekiel has it: 'Feed your stomach and fill your body with this scroll which I am giving you. Then I ate it, and it was sweet as honey in my mouth.'

That takes it a lot more seriously than we usually do at Friday night dinner, and as a gentile, while I respect the spiritual significance, I mainly enjoy the cake.

Lekach is a vital part of the Rosh Hashanah new year feast, and cruel commentators often note that a brick of home-made honey cake is present at that celebration to be observed and admired, rather than eaten.

Certainly an ill-made honey cake is a dry, heavy thing, difficult to love even if it has been made by your mother; but a proper honey cake, like Panzer's or Lisa Dangoor's, is never dry... and we like to serve it with a scoop of honey ice cream for those that wish to ease it down the throat.

The tendency to dryness in honey cake is well known, but there are many alternative solutions for those who baulk at ice cream. At Honey & Co, the wonderful Bloomsbury Middle Eastern restaurant, husband and wife chefs Sarit Packer and Itamar Srulovich's signature dish is a feta and honey cheesecake on a kadaif pastry base that is a long way from lekach but infinitely lickable.

Honey & Co is a Middle Eastern restaurant rather than a specifically Jewish restaurant, and the Sephardic branch of Judaism and its spicy, colourful cuisine has a lot in common with the Arabic traditions that prevail to the south of my home, along the Edgware Road as it leads into central London.

This has always been an important route in London. For the Romans it was the main road north from the little city they built next to the Thames, and over the centuries it became the start of the Great North Road – even now it transitions into the M1, the original motorway out of the capital.

In medieval and Tudor times huge crowds flocked south along it to witness public executions at Tyburn, the southern terminus of the road, now known as Marble Arch and drawing crowds almost as vast, if less bloodthirsty, to the retail temples of Selfridges and Primark.

Throughout my half century and more as a Londoner – and indeed for fifty years before that – the area has been a magnet for immigrants from the Levant and the Middle East, initially from Egypt and Iraq, then Algeria, the Lebanon and many other Arab-speaking nations.

All of these people of course brought their food with them and established restaurants that, in the time-honoured London fashion, replaced those of preceding waves of immigrants – we have already seen how the spot that once housed

London's pre-eminent baker of Battenberg cake is now a large and thriving Lebanese café.

At the top of the dessert list on the menu there at Al Arez – and at just about every other café and restaurant on the Edgware Road, regardless of nationality – is baklawa, the mother of all Middle Eastern sweet treats, made with pastry, nuts and honey. Or is it actually made with syrup? And should it really be spelt baklava?

It is a complex and confusing matter. The muddle is well summed up by the *Encyclopaedia Britannica*, which goes with the 'v' and suggests that this is 'phyllo' pastry with nuts, honey and lemon juice that can be additionally flavoured with cardamom and rosewater in the syrup, and that it comes from Turkey, Greece and the Middle East. That certainly covers all bases.

For greater clarity, I consulted the veteran waiters at Lemonia, just down the road, who have been serving fine Greek food to hungry north-west Londoners for decades. It's baklava, they said, quite definitely; it is Greek and it is made with filo pastry, nuts, spices and honey. Always honey.

The experts at Sweetland London, who have been making Lebanese sweets in my area for a quarter of a century, agree that the Greek version uses honey, as does the Turkish, differing only in preferring pistachios while the Greeks favour walnuts. But Lebanese bakers, they say, or those from the Middle East in general, use sugar syrup, not honey, flavoured with orange blossom or rosewater. The spelling, I can tell you, doesn't really matter, because any English spelling is a transliteration either from Greek or Arabic.

The point as far as this chapter is concerned is that it is an ancient cake, or pastry, or sweet, often made with honey. The honey version, countless layers of filo pastry dripping with the sweet stuff and further enriched with chopped nuts, is sensational with a strong coffee or a fresh mint tea at the end of a long summer lunch. I love the soft crunch and chewiness, the sweet decadence, the ritual of licking fingers after each little oblong. It is a precious treat.

In structure, if not in flavour, baklava has a lot in common with Russian honey cake – all those layers.

Just over the road from our house is Raoul's, a deli and *traiteur* where the prices are almost comically high but the sourcing of stock and cooking of the meals to take away are imaginative and highly competent. Raoul's always has in stock a tray of the other kind of honey cake that we adore, the Russian version known as medovik.

This is a different prospect altogether from the ancient simplicity of the lekach: multiple layers of honey-enriched egg dough sandwiching sour cream and topped with the ground trimmings of the layers; the dough requiring careful attention in a bain-marie and the assembly of the final cake a challenge to the most dextrous of bakers.

When cut, revealing close-packed stripes of dough and cream, it is a most striking item, and there are those who make it who will tell you it has an equally striking history.

Medovik, the story goes, was first created in the early years of the nineteenth century by the personal chef of Elizaveta Alekseevna, wife of the Russian Emperor Alexander I, and – weirdly, given its ingredients – it was called into being for someone who didn't like honey.

The palace cooks, we are told, knew of the Empress's foible, and never used honey in their recipes – presumably being well able to afford sugar instead.

But then along came a thrusting young chef who was new to royal service and wanted to make a name for himself. There was a competition among the palace cooks to create a new dessert dish, and the young chef's creation, featuring thin layers of sweet dough and cream, took the fancy of the Empress.

The great lady called the young chef to her and asked what had gone into this delightful dish. At first he refused to answer, but eventually revealed the contents of the cake, fearing that he would be expelled from royal service or flung into a dungeon for his impudence.

But instead the Empress laughed, praised his bravery and ordered that he should be rewarded. The layered honey cake was added to all future banqueting menus as a favourite of the hostess.

Isn't it a great story? It has all the elements of a blockbuster, or a pantomime: royalty, daring, suspense and reward. It is such a good story that it is told about other cakes, too, the Imperial Cake of Austria, for example and, more poignantly at the time of writing, the Kiev Cake of Ukraine.

In fact, as the *Moscow Times* (a reliable independent source) has pointed out, there is no evidence for a cake of this kind in

Russia in the early nineteenth century: 'We can't find any special honey cakes in any cookbook of the early nineteenth century,' the publication declares. 'We checked "The Cooking, Serving, Confection Making and Distilling Dictionary" (1795– 1797) by Vasily Levshin; I. Navrotsky's the "New Complete Cookbook" (1808), "The General Complete and Expert Confectioner" (1811) – nowhere are honey cakes mentioned. The fashion for them would not come to Russia until almost a century later.'

The tale of the Tsarina's courageous cook, in short, is an invention, an early example of cake-related fake news.

It seems that the cake first truly became popular not in the palatial cooking quarters of the Tsar – any Tsar – but in the humble kitchens of Soviet citizens in the twentieth century. Some go so far as to claim that the first mention of a recipe for the cake is not in an imperial archive but in a book of Ukrainian recipes published, in Ukrainian, in 1960...

Certainly it is true that medovik has become an immensely popular dish in Russia, and as restaurants in that country attempted to appeal to a wealthier clientele in the early years of this century, the relatively humble ingredients of the 'national cake' were augmented with plutocratic embellishments: the simple sour cream filling replaced by exotic caramels, the garnish – no more than crumbled offcuts in the original – with shards of honeycomb, twirls of meringue and chocolate truffles, the whole thing enveloped in gold leaf...

The version we enjoy at home is free from any such nonsense: it comes from Raoul's deli over the road, a popular spot with Russian families who live in vast but discreet mansions over the main road in St John's Wood, and who have become even more discreet since the invasion of Ukraine.

The cake is intricate and delicate, and no matter how experienced the pâtissier it takes – I am assured – a long time to cook and assemble. The lady who serves our slices, sliding a spatula under them with infinite care, so as not to crumple the bottom layer, tells me that it is almost impossible to cut the cake when it is freshly made, as the layers slide about on one another.

The best approach – the only approach, she insists – is to let the cake settle for an hour, then refrigerate it overnight, and only then cut it, with an extremely sharp knife. This allows the layers of dough to soak up some, but not all, of the frosting, and the whole to cohere and solidify. But not for too long, as this demanding cake, which cannot be eaten too soon after creation, also does not keep well, because the outer layers of dough can harden and suggest staleness.

So there is a sweet spot: it is best served for lunch on the day after the evening on which it was made. Not the kind of thing that you rustle up at a moment's notice, whether you are chef to a Tsar or a Soviet Commissar.

And it is not the kind of thing that you serve in large quantities. A slice of medovik from Raoul's is stunningly expensive, but I have found that a single slice can be quartered for serving with successful results. So rich is the cake, so sweet and creamy and satisfying, that a cube 5cm square, served with a handful of berries, makes a delightful dessert.

I should point out that there are home-grown, entirely English versions of honey cake that have been created in this land as long as people have had grains and honey to mix and cook. If only we had got the hang of wall-painting, there might be records of Somerset honey cake from the time of the Pharoahs.

In the east of England, in particular, there are local recipes for honey cake that produce solid, thin results a lot like soft biscuits, cousins of the honey cakes from the Low Countries over the water, where such items often have stamped decorations and are associated with religious festivals.

Often, in eastern England as in the Netherlands and Belgium, these are flavoured with spices as well as honey; add a little ginger, and of course you have gingerbread, closely related to honey cake and worthy of a chapter all on its own – except that it is a bread, or a biscuit, and therefore falls outside my strict rules of engagement.

I know of plenty of less biscuity English honey cakes that are highly satisfactory, including one from Middlesex that adds orange peel, ginger and cinnamon to a pound cake base mix; one from Somerset that bakes whole slices of local apples into the mix, adding a moist fruitiness.

There is rarely debate in my household about what will conclude our Sunday lunches when guests are expected. It will certainly be honey cake: the only question is, which one? Sometimes we choose according to the guests we are expecting and their known or predicted tastes.

Sometimes the choice is dictated by what we have available to serve alongside the honey cake: the medovik, as I have said, is best dished up with berries in season; the lekach needs honey ice cream (kosher, if required for some guests: honey stirred into bought kosher vanilla ice cream and re-frozen); baklava demands, I feel, strong coffee or fragrant tea.

So it is difficult to nominate a single True Slice from the trio. Perhaps it is best to say that the true slice of honey cake is a slice of the cake that is most appropriate to the guests that we are welcoming. At least there is no quibbling over the authenticity of the location: it is my home.

Because this is where the journey, and the story, ends: with a slice of lekach, made to a family recipe, on a plate that my daughter made in pottery class twenty years ago.

I've travelled the length and breadth of the country eating cake, to the far north and deep south, to east and west, and the story which began in the remembered kitchen of my childhood concludes in the kitchen of my here and now.

Honey cake helps to draw together and focus some of the thoughts about cake which have been prompted by my travels. For instance, the constant debate about origin and attribution, evident with honey cake and with many of the other cakes that I have tasted, so often a talisman of some kind, representing a geographical area, a shared heritage or set of beliefs.

When people defend their cake, whether it is one named after their community, or their local or family version of a well-known cake, they are not just saying that their recipe is better than anyone else's, they are expressing pride in where they come from and who they are, and joy in being able to share something that in a way represents who they are.

They are all, individually, correct: their version is true to them... which means, I have learned, that a quest for the True Slice of any cake, while useful as a discipline for a restless explorer or curious writer, is ultimately doomed. Not only are there endless variations of a recipe, but every time a cake goes into the oven, no matter how faithfully the instructions have been followed, the result will be subtly different from every previous version of that cake. Perhaps the most important thing I learned was not to be judgmental, but to enjoy the little differences, savour the nuances.

Because this is how cake has evolved down the years, through experiment, disaster and happy accident, from the incinerated oatcakes of King Alfred to the wild innovations of the *Bake Off* tent, inherited recipes tweaked for new generations, old ways enhanced by new technology.

The results, even if less than perfect, can always be shared. Cake inspires generosity, and I quickly lost count of the number of times that people I met to discuss their local cake offered me an extra chunk to take home... not that it always got there.

People everywhere, I was delighted to find, love to share a slice of their lives, and I'd share a slice of this honey cake with you, if I could. Here is the recipe, the final recipe, instead...

HONEY CAKE

This is a family recipe: it comes from my cousin-in-law, Lisa Dangoor, who has an online shop at cakeitwithlisa.com. Lisa puts a witty spin on traditional recipes, but this has generations of love and ancient lore at heart.

Lisa says: 'One of my favourite Jewish traditions is making sweet food for Rosh Hashanah, the Jewish new year, to mark the introduction of a sweet year ahead. Honey is the most typical sweet ingredient to use due to its association with the manna in the Torah and its availability to our ancestors. Although I am a Sephardic Jew, I like to branch out into recipes from other streams of Judaism, allowing me to learn about other cultures through a culinary lens. This exploration led me to discover lekach, a delicious Ashkenazi honey cake originating in Germany which has been adapted all over the world.'

BACK HOME: HONEY CAKE

2 eggs

190g caster sugar

250g honey

2 tbsp brandy or rum (use lemon juice as an alcohol-free alternative)

130ml vegetable oil

120ml black coffee, cooled

300g plain flour

2½ tsp baking powder

2 tsp ground cinnamon

½ tsp ground cloves

½ tsp ground nutmeg

zest of 1 orange, finely grated

a pinch of salt

50g dried fruit, e.g. sultanas (optional)

50g chopped walnuts and/or slivered almonds (optional)

1. Preheat the oven to 190°C/375°F/Gas Mark 5.
2. In a large bowl, beat the eggs and caster sugar until pale in colour, then add the honey and whisk to combine.
3. Slowly pour in the brandy/rum or lemon juice, vegetable oil and black coffee while whisking and continue to whisk until the ingredients are fully combined to form a smooth mixture.
4. In a separate bowl, combine the flour, baking powder, spices, orange zest and salt.
5. Add the dry ingredients to the wet in three parts, folding to combine between each addition.

6. If you are using dried fruit and nuts, toss them in flour before adding them to prevent them from sinking to the bottom of the cake, then fold them into the mixture.

7. Transfer the mixture to a greased loaf or bundt tin and bake in the oven for about an hour, or until a toothpick is inserted into the centre and comes out clean.

8. Leave to cool and cut into slices to serve.

ACKNOWLEDGEMENTS

First of all, to Ingrid, Lucy and Emily, and Sammy the dog, who held the fort at home while I charged around the country on what must have seemed self-indulgent missions: thank you for all the support, love and patience, and I'm sorry that so few slices made it home.

Big thanks to Charlie Redmayne of HarperCollins, for the initial opportunity and several excellent lunches, and especially to his inspiring colleagues Katya Shipster and the heroic Cyan Turan for immensely positive, painstaking and perceptive editorial support, to Sarah Hammond for meticulous project editing skills and to Simon Armstrong for marketing wizardry. I consider myself very fortunate to have benefited from Becca Thorne's delicious illustrations; and heartfelt plaudits too to Becky Ritchie and Tom Killingbeck at A. M. Heath for doing the tricky stuff and allowing me to focus on the words. A giant herogram to my friend Alice Whately, who did a very great deal of extremely useful research, chasing red herrings and tracking down elusive facts.

Love and thanks to my mother, for her many reminiscences of the cakes of my youth (and hers), and to her friends in Letcombe Regis, notably the wonderfully helpful Ann and Paul, and Martin and the Richmond Letcombe Regis catering team (who make a very good Chocolate Nemesis).

Huge thanks to my brother James, fellow scourge of the childhood fête cake stalls, and to my cousin Janie and her husband Graeme, who invited me to be part of their lovely wedding – and allowed me to write about it. To Kathryn and Stuart Sanders, for their incredible patience in countless discussions of cakes and destinations; and to Jeremy and Anna Sanders, and Jonathan and Tina Sanders for upbeat advice; and special thanks to my Instagram advisors and regular culinary consultants Naomi and David Crossland.

I benefited from the kindness of many friends who bake much better than I ever will, and whose knowledge of cakes in general and area-specific cakes in particular saved me from multiple howlers. Those mistakes that remain, I hasten to add, are my responsibility entirely.

Many of those experts who helped me are mentioned in the text, but I am also indebted to many others for all kinds of information and assistance, including: Lauren Dall of Dundee's Master Bakers; Amy Hulyer and Emma Gough at English Heritage; Hannah Berry from the Wolseley; Melissa Thompson; Ruth Burke-Kennedy at Bettys; Anni Ahonen at Sister London on behalf of the Hummingbird Bakery; David, Bobbi, Amy and Sophie at Marks & Spencer; Max Scotford and all at Bullion in Sheffield; Toby Hampton, Claire Burnet and the Chococo team; and Natasha and Lisa Dangoor.

ACKNOWLEDGEMENTS

I'd also like to thank my colleagues at the *Telegraph* for advice and encouragement, in particular our brilliant food editor Amy Bryant, and my Lifestyle teammates Tomé Morrissy-Swan, Keith Miller, Victoria Young, Caroline Barrett-Haigh, Boudicca Fox-Leonard, Jack Rear, Alexis Giles, Lizzie Frainier, Jessica Doyle, Caroline Knell, Jade Conroy and McKenna Grant, with special shout-outs to Sharon Walker, Maddi Howell and Tom Ough, and commendations for Amber Dalton, Paul Hudson, Steve Davis, Charlotte Braunagel, Angela Connell, Anna Murfet and Kath Brown. Ace columnist and tremendous novelist Sophia Money-Coutts was generous with time and advice and is an excellent lunch companion. Bryony Gordon was totally brilliant and kind in many ways, and Avril Ormsby supplied cupcakes and smiles at crucial moments.

Away from the office, Clarissa Vallat was supportive, knowledgeable and very good with ducks; and Alison Nagle, Lizzy Gillett, Simona Negretto, Eliza Thompson, Imogen Lycett-Green, Annalisa Barbieri, Amelia Rope and Meg Roberts provided constructive advice, encouragement, lunch and hot chocolate (in no particular order). Special awards to Ben, Minnow and Lizzie for neighbourliness; and I would like to thank my Twitter pals Louise Venter, @Ruffbinta (Kelly Woods) and Eva (@croissant1226).

Elmer and the Tuesday Night Crew know how important they are: I can't thank them by name, but they are indispensable.

The recipes in this book remain the copyright of their authors: Eccles cake, Felicity Cloake; Dundee cake, the Master Bakers of Dundee; Victoria sandwich, English Heritage;

CAKE

Battenberg cake, Rose Prince; Christmas cake, Xanthe Clay;
Wedding cake, Lucy Netherton; Ginger parkin, Bettys; Red
velvet cupcakes, the Hummingbird Bakery; Chocolate biscuit
cake, Chococo; Geometric jewel cake, the Big Bake; Lekach
honey cake, Lisa Dangoor.